THE CO

With many thanks

+

And wishes

Nicky G.

Nov '96

THE COLLECTION

edited by Mark Elsdon-Dew

HTB PUBLICATIONS

LONDON

Unless otherwise indicated, biblical quotations
are from either the Good News Version © 1994 by the
American Bible Society, or the New International Version,
© 1973, 1978, 1984 by the International Bible Society.

ISBN 1-898838-29-1

Front cover illustration by Charlie Mackesy

Editor's Acknowledgements

I am profoundly grateful to all this book's contributors, who never
expected their spoken words to be put into print, but have given me
immense encouragement with this project. I would also like to thank
Gil Rea, Tanya Ivas and Linda Williams for all their help with typing,
editing and honing the final manuscript.

Designed and produced by Bookprint Creative Services
P.O. Box 827, BN21 3YJ, England for
HTB PUBLICATIONS
Brompton Road, London, SW7 1JA
Printed in Great Britain.

CONTENTS

3. Faith's challenges

4. The mission of the Church

5. The power of the Spirit

The teachings of the wise are a fountain of life...

Proverbs 13 v14

BIOGRAPHIES

John Arnott
Senior pastor of the Toronto Airport Christian Fellowship, a church which has seen a remarkable move of the Holy Spirit in recent years, attracting visitors from all over the world.

Michael Cassidy
The founder of African Enterprise and one of the most influential Christian leaders in southern Africa, Michael Cassidy is author of several books including *Bursting the Wineskins* and *A Witness For Ever.*

Steve Chalke
International Director of Oasis Trust, a charitable trust involved in church and social work in Britain and abroad, Steve Chalke is a Baptist minister who presents regularly on television.

Pastor David Yonggi Cho
Leader of the world's largest church in Seoul, Korea, Pastor Cho is a leading authority on prayer and has written several books on the subject.

Michael Coates
A former headmaster of Monkton Combe Junior School and Secretary of the Incorporated Association of Preparatory Schools, Michael Coates is a lay reader in the Anglican church.

John Collins
Former Vicar of St Mark's, Gillingham, Canford and Holy Trinity Brompton. John Collins is retired and lives in Oxford.

Ken Costa
Chairman of the Investment Banking Board of merchant bankers SBC Warburg, Ken Costa is a senior financier in the city. He is also the founder of the READY vision to inspire and equip young Christians.

Gordon Fee
Professor of New Testament at Regent College, Vancouver, in Canada, Gordon Fee is author of numerous theological works, including a much-heralded commentary of 1 Corinthians. He has recently published a comprehensive book on Paul's treatment of the Holy Spirit in his epistles entitled *God's Empowering Presence* (Paternoster Press).

Richard Foster
Bestselling author of *Prayer: Finding the Heart's True Home* and *Celebration of Discipline*, Richard Foster is the founder of *RENOVARÉ*, a movement commited to spiritual renewal.

Tom Gillum
A former Chaplain to the Royal Brompton Hospital, Tom Gillum is Priest-in-Charge of St Stephen's Church, Westbourne Park, which was 'planted' from Holy Trinity Brompton in 1994.

Jeremy Jennings
Pastoral Director of Holy Trinity Brompton for the last ten years, Jeremy Jennings has led the growth of corporate prayer in the church for the past six years.

J. John
One of the most popular evangelists in Britain today, with a cross-denominational acceptability, J. John travels all over the country and the world speaking about Jesus Christ. He is author of several books

including *Dead Sure?*, *Natural Evangelism* and the best-selling *What's the Point of Christmas?*

John McClure

John McClure is Senior Pastor of the Vineyard Christian Fellowship in Newport Beach, California.

Sandy Millar

A former barrister, Sandy Millar has been Vicar of Holy Trinity Brompton for 11 years. He has considerable experience of church planting and has led a large number of Alpha and church leadership conferences.

Paul Negrut

Persecuted under the Ceausescu regime, Paul Negrut is pastor of the Second Baptist Church in Oradea, Romania, and President of the Romanian Evangelical Alliance.

Lesslie Newbigin

Lesslie Newbigin served as a missionary in India from 1936 to 1974 with a break of six years from '59 to '65 when he was Secretary of the International Missionary Council and then Associate Secretary of the World Council of Churches. He was one of the Bishops consecrated in 1947 at the inauguration of the Church of South India. He is the author of several books including *The Gospel in a Pluralist Society*.

Steve Nicholson

Steve Nicholson is Senior Pastor of the Vineyard Christian Fellowship, Evanston, Illinois, USA.

James Odgers

James Odgers is a merchant banker and founder of the Besom Foundation, which provides a bridge between those who want to give money, time or skills, and those who are in need.

Nick and Jane Oundjian

Three years after the tragic death of their 13-month-old-son Jeremy 17 years ago from a sudden illness, Nick and Jane Oundjian became committed Christians. They run a bereavement course at Holy Trinity Brompton and Jane Oundjian is a trained counsellor with the national bereavement agency CRUSE.

David Parker

David Parker is Senior Pastor of the Vineyard Christian Fellowship in Lancaster, California.

Jackie Pullinger-To

Jackie Pullinger-To has been a missionary in Hong Kong since 1966 and is the founder of the St Stephen's Society. Her work with heroin addicts in the colony's notorious Walled City has brought recognition throughout the world and is described in her best-selling book *Chasing the Dragon*.

Glenda Waddell

Glenda Waddell is a member of the staff of Holy Trinity Brompton, where she is actively involved in the church's prayer ministry.

John Wimber

Leader and founder of the Association of Vineyard Churches, John Wimber is one of the foremost authorities on church growth in the world. He has led numerous conferences worldwide on a variety of topics including healing, the gifts of the Holy Spirit, church growth, signs and wonders, prayer and power evangelism. He has received treatment for cancer in recent years and is now recovering.

Chris Woods

Chris Woods is Vicar of Holy Trinity, Parr Mount, St Helens, Merseyside, an urban priority area in the north of England.

FOREWORD

by Sandy Millar

The Collection is an unusual book. Mark Elsdon-Dew has taken teaching from many different sources (most of those whose teaching is included here would almost certainly be unknown to one another) but all speak of the same eternal, unchangingly faithful, generous and loving God who has chosen to reveal himself to us through his Son Jesus Christ. Not in super success-stories as the world would see them, but in the realities of relationship and day-to-day life, difficulties and persecution, sadness, sickness and bereavement.

All those who have contributed to this book are personal friends of ours here at Holy Trinity Brompton. They each in their different ways bring their own experience and giftedness to their teaching. They each have a passion for Jesus Christ and it is this rather than the attempt to make the immediacy of their spoken teaching look like polished prose that, in my view, holds it all so powerfully together. I hope you will find it as helpful and inspiring as I have.

INTRODUCTION

by Mark Elsdon-Dew

Whether by virtue of its unique situation in the centre of London, its large congregation, or its position as a resourcing church and the home of the popular 'Alpha Course', a large variety of well-known teachers and speakers have accepted invitations to speak at Holy Trinity Brompton or at one of its events.

During the last five years, I have published edited extracts of some of the material in the church's monthly newspaper *Focus*. Although some talks were reproduced at length, my intention was mainly to select bits and pieces which I had found personally most moving and helpful.

This book is a collection of those extracts and I must acknowledge my gratitude to all the contributors for giving me permission not only to 'pick and choose', but to go ahead and print their words which, when delivered, were never intended for publication.

The result, I hope you will agree, is a book which is not only a fascinating and stimulating collection of teaching material, but a medley which can be dipped into time and again to encourage us in what Paul refers to as the 'good fight of the faith'.

Walking in Faith

"We have been drawn... to a sincere and pure devotion to Christ."

Sandy Millar *on living the Christian life*

> I am afraid that ... your minds may somehow be led astray from your sincere and pure devotion to Christ. (2 Corinthians 11:3)

The call of God is a strange thing. You start to analyse it and you get lost. You try to describe it to an old friend who is outside the kingdom of God and he looks blank and suggests a game of golf next Sunday. Nevertheless, it is a real and precious thing. It is the stirring in every part of us – mind, body, soul and spirit – in response to the overwhelming love of God.

Jesus spoke to Nicodemus about the wind, "blowing wherever it pleases. You hear its sound but you cannot tell where it comes from or where it is going. So it is with everyone born of the Spirit." Nicodemus looked blank too because until then it hadn't happened to him and he couldn't therefore see the kingdom of God.

For some it is a gradual realisation; for some quite a sudden thing (there are examples in the Bible of both) but in all of us who have been born from above, something distinctive has happened. Paul describes it beautifully in this part of his letter to the people whom he loved so deeply in Corinth. We have been drawn, he says, to a sincere and pure devotion to Christ.

The problem that Paul faced in Corinth was that there were

strong voices within the Church there that were seeking to seduce it. They were doubtless very 'modern' and 'liberal', but they were preaching their own version of Christianity and the beguiling subtlety with which they were unsettling the Christians there, drew from Paul some of his most anguished teaching yet.

For the call of God was then, and still is, a call to a sincere and pure devotion to Christ. The difficulty faced by those who have heard that call and responded to it, is that those outside the kingdom of God simply do not – and Jesus said 'cannot' – understand why devotion to Christ carries with it a passion for Jesus Christ himself, for his honour, for everything that he said and a desire to respond to his slightest wish.

That is simply another way of saying that to be brought within sound of the voice of God is to be profoundly altered. It is to have one's centre of gravity radically changed, all because we have begun to understand the true implications of redemption; not only the horror of the cross but also the dawning realisation that what God the Father was doing (and Jesus Christ with him) was something so wonderfully sacrificial and unconditionally generous that it draws from us the desire to be what he wants us to be and do what he wants us to do.

We have seen through supernatural eyes that he alone is real, and have begun also increasingly to see the grubbiness and inadequacy of so many aspects of the old life from which Jesus died to save us.

To you, the church of Christ here, I want to provide these reflections.

Life in the kingdom of God is always going to be different from the life of the world. We ought not expect people outside the kingdom of God to be able to live up to the standards of morality, sexuality or honesty that are set before those in the kingdom of God. Our call from God is to tell them about Jesus Christ, to show them by our lives a better way and serve them as servants of Christ for his sake, in any way we can. He loves them and wants all to be saved.

The Church has always been called to purity for God's nature is to be pure. That means purity of thought and deed; relationships that are open and honest. Sexual activity (hetero or homo) outside marriage destroys that precious 'sincere and pure devotion to Christ', and marriage is one man, one woman, for life. In our hearts we know that and in our hearts we are right.

Jesus set a standard that even condemned lustful thoughts but we have been subjected in recent times to so many confusing arguments – a sort of drip feed of a different brand of so-called Christianity, a 'Christianity' without the cross, in which self-denial plays no part, an anaemic unsatisfying brand of Christ-less religion in which 'I' am at the centre and God on the fringe – that we have lost sight of the pursuit of holiness. But we are committed to God's point of view, and sympathy for God's point of view is what seems to be lacking in many parts of Christ's church today. Church leaders are called to lead and any attempt to buy off any party with specious sub-biblical or heretical views can only lead, in the long run to the deep discouragement and ultimate disaffection of the loyal flock who are trying to lead a biblically Christian life against fierce opposition from the world, the flesh and the devil.

That is why it is serious, as well as sad, when leaders fall and when they do they must lay down their leadership responsibility. That too is why leaders must teach clearly and unambiguously. Of course practising homosexuals should not be ordained. Of course those in Christian leadership who are involved in immoral relationships (hetero or homo) should resign or be removed. It can sadly happen all too easily but it is inconsistent with Christian leadership. This is nothing to do with homophobia – it is to do with a proper phobia of sin. A so-called 'stable relationship' that is immoral is, after all, only one that has gone on for longer than any other one.

All of that leads me to this: sometime, in some place, there has to be a body of people who are committed to living out the life of Christ, in sincere and pure devotion to him, reaching out to the people of the world in his name to offer them not criticism, but a better way of life and an unconditional love through an incomparable Saviour. They have traditionally been called the Church. In this generation why shouldn't they be us?

"The tiniest bit of faith in the right object is sufficient."

John McClure *on biblical faith*

I think some people feel that if they just had enough faith that would get them through. But it's not a question of having a massive quantity of faith. You can have massive faith in a rickety chair that will not support you and go over. Sit on it and it will crash down. But you need only the tiniest wit of faith in a concrete floor – if you put out your toe and try it and find that it will support you, then walk on it, pretty soon you realise you can run and jump on it. Just a little bit of faith in a concrete floor is sufficient.

You can stand on top of a building ten stories up, convince yourself that you can fly, and say, "Well, here I go" and dive off, flapping your arms. I tell you, you'll just drop like a brick! It doesn't matter how much faith you have – you can be loaded with faith – you will just make a terrible mess.

But on the other hand you need only the tiniest bit of faith in a 747 – if you can just muscle up the faith to get in the door and buckle yourself in, you can go all the way to London and you'll be fine. The tiniest bit of faith in the right object is sufficient.

Biblical faith is just taking the tiniest bit of faith and putting it in the right object – that is Jesus Christ – and saying, "I trust you!"

"He had a big piece of straw in the corner of his mouth and he was leaning back and just floating down the river!"

John McClure *on faith in times of trouble*

As a kid, our family used to take vacations at the end of summer when we went to Yellowstone National Park in Wyoming. It was always a wonderful trip for us. We would pull a trailer and have a boat on top of the car, and the whole family would have a wonderful two weeks.

I remember one time on the road, along the Snake River which is in Idaho – a vast beautiful river about 100 yards across – we were driving when a great electrical storm struck. After a while, we became afraid of going on, so my dad pulled into a sheltered area and we all went back and sat in the trailer. We began counting the strikes of lightning, and then of course the thunder that would come along afterwards. I remember we counted over 100 as we watched the lightning striking everywhere. There was such violence all around us, it was really quite frightening.

We glanced over to the river and we saw a little object that looked very strange out there. As it got closer we realised it was a massive inner tube from the tyre of an airplane, floating slowly down the river. As it got nearer to us, we finally realised there was a huge fat man sitting on this airplane inner tube.

He must have been wearing swimming trunks because otherwise he was just out there large as life. It was a warm summer day and I remember he was wearing a great big hat and he had a big piece of straw in the corner of his mouth and he was leaning back and just floating down the river!

I'll never forget that sight. With lightning striking everywhere and thunder peals all over, here was this man floating by – he looked over and saw us and he just waved, and all of us waved back to him. He just floated on by!

I've never forgotten that picture, because that's what your life is supposed to be like in the midst of all the trauma, all the lightning and all the stress, pressure and struggle. Your life is supposed to have that bit of grass coming out of your mouth and that hat on your head, and you are literally flowing along in the stream of the Spirit of God.

"But I will never forget... the look on the face of Jesus – that marvellous, sympathetic look of absolute power and yet such pathos, such tenderness..."

John McClure *describes how God revealed to him that David Watson, the British evangelist, was going to die*

I will never forget seeing the throne of grace in December of 1983. David Watson was dying of cancer and he flew over to

Los Angeles. I remember getting a phone call in the morning from John Wimber saying, "John, I want you to come up and join me. David has come over for prayer and I wonder if you could set this day aside." So I did. I changed my plans, drove over and I remember we spent the day in John's office with David just praying over him.

At about 3 o'clock in the afternoon when someone was praying, I had a vision. It is one of the privileges of my life that I have the occasional, often very vivid vision. But this was certainly the most vivid vision I had ever had in my life.

Suddenly I was taken up out of the room and I found myself in a great ante-room. It was a magnificent room and it seemed to have a glass floor, as though we were standing on clouds. It was just a beautiful, beautiful room. We were all together waiting there.

David was there and John, and several of the others who were praying for him. We were all standing chatting with each other and at the end of the room, there were two great doors. After a while the doors opened and two great angels walked in and beckoned us to come. We turned and went with them through the doors and suddenly, we were in a room that was so massive I couldn't tell you the dimensions of it. It seemed like 100 miles across except somehow, you could see the whole room. It was a vast amphitheatre, a theatre on all sides and it looked like millions of people were inside worshipping and praising the Lord. There were angels above and in the centre was this magnificent throne. Over it was a great rainbow of glory, just radiant. It didn't matter where you were, it looked the same from every side.

There was one seated on this throne that you could hardly look at. But it seemed like 50 miles away and I remember just glancing at it. Suddenly, these angels took us and we were there in front of the throne of grace! It was absolutely awesome – beyond words to describe.

I remember that we carried David up the stairs of this throne and Jesus stood up, came down the stairs and met us half way. We lifted David into his arms and he turned and walked back, and we walked down. Suddenly, we were in the ante-room again and then I was back in the prayer room. It was a couple of days later that I woke in the middle of the night and realised that we had left David there.

I picked up the phone and called John the next day and said, "You know in that vision, I realise that the Lord was telling me that David was going to be going home." On February 18, 1984, he passed into the presence of the Lord.

I will never forget that throne, or the look on the face of Jesus – that marvellous, sympathetic look of absolute power and yet such pathos, such tenderness – so completely engaged in the struggle that David was in.

"The well meaning people were saying, 'You've got to normalise. You've got to put more devotional time in with the kids.' I never was good at devotions. I mean I was devoted but I was never good at organising devotions."

John Wimber *on faith and his family*

I was converted out of the pagan pool and had very little understanding of church life. For four generations, we had nobody in my family with any identification with a church. As a new Christian, I found that other Christians would come to me and say, "You're spending too much time with the unsaved. You're spending night after night winning people to Christ. You must raise your children," and I said, "Well, I agree with that but I thought I was."

You see, I was spending time with the unsaved but I was doing it in my living room with my children on my lap. We never said, "Now, children, go out of the room. We have something important to talk about here." We talked about it and over them to the visitor. If we had to cast out a demon, or pray for the sick, lend money to someone who needed it, or take someone in, we did it.

We had people living with us for 20 years. Our children never resented that. They still refer to those people as 'aunts' and 'uncles' and friends and loved ones. They still tell stories: "Dad, do you remember when we went out and started that church in that garage and how funny it was? Remember that time when we went to the mission and that man came up who was drunk and you talked to him and he got sober? Remember when we went to the jail and they wouldn't let me in and you wouldn't go in unless I could go in. They let us both in and you prayed for those people and they became Christians? Do you remember those Bible studies?"

You know, my kids never ever saw a difference between the way we were publicly and the way we were privately. We were never very 'religious' if religious means affected. We were always broke, always trusting God and always in trouble and somebody always hated us.

The well meaning people were saying, "You've got to normalise. You've got to put more devotional time in with the kids." I never was good at devotions. I mean I was devoted but I was never good at organising devotions. I would try to tell the Bible stories and the kids would get bored. I would try to read the booklets and they didn't like those either.

But they loved seeing illustrations – the living illustrations of the same thing. They remember when the demons came out of 'that man'. They were young but they remember watching it and praying with me. One of them remembers in the midst of a long deliverance session, there was a big bag of potato chips and I was hungry, so I was casting the demons out and eating the potato chips at the same time. They thought it was funny. I didn't know you weren't supposed to do that. It doesn't say anything about it in the Bible.

If we didn't have any money we said so. If we didn't have any faith we said so. But we said it first to God and then he would give it to us. If we didn't have the money for a vacation or holiday, we just said so: "Hey kids, we're not going to go anywhere unless God does something for us," and when he did something for us we were all very grateful. He did it over and over again.

We didn't go out and tell anybody, "Oh, we're living by faith and it just isn't working out too well. Pray for us, brother." God told us not to do that. That's manipulative. So we didn't do that. But what we did do is we never told anyone a lie. We never pretended that things were different from what they were. We never quit doing it and we never will until Jesus comes.

> *"When children ask us if they may do something, there are only two answers: either 'No' or 'Yes, willingly'. The answer we are so tempted to give, but which we should never give is: 'Yes, grudgingly.'"*

Michael Coates *on parenting*

There's a mistake that we commonly make which is to confuse two things: compromise on the one hand and balance on the other. Compromise is a quality which is traditionally highly regarded by our nation. 'A good British compromise' we say. In matters of policy, compromise is right and admirable. It's not however suitable in matters of ethics or morality or behaviour or belief.

In education, upbringing and other aspects of our lives we need not compromise but balance, where we hold in tension two points that may seem opposite and even contradictory and, without attempting to reconcile them, we find a way between the two.

We teach our children to play games. On the one hand, they must play flat out to win, with no half-heartedness. On the other, they must be sportsmanlike, with no ruthlessness. No half-heartedness, no ruthlessness – that is a difficult concept, difficult enough for adults as you can see sometimes from your television screens, very difficult for children. You are refereeing a rugby match and a voice comes out of the scrum,"Go on, kill him." You blow the whistle, disentangle the players, identify the culprit, and you are met with an expression of innocent blankness: "But you said I was to be whole-hearted." Another time, as you watch from the touch-line the vital moment of a match, one of the three-quarters stands aside as if to say to the other side, "Go on – your turn." Afterwards you remonstrate. Again the blank look: "But you said I was to be sportsmanlike." The answer is that it's both. Not a mixture of the two, which is the worst of both worlds – but both. We want them to be wholly committed and wholly sportsmanlike.

Now may I follow this on to some other examples. Take love and firmness. Before I was a parent myself, I thought it was a sensible question to ask parents which child they loved the most. Once I became a parent I realised that the question is meaningless. Parents love all their children totally. If we have two children, it doesn't mean that each child has half our love, or that four children have a quarter each. All our children have all our love – which incidentally, is a picture of God's love for us.

Then what about firmness? What do we do when we have to deny our children something that love would like to give to them? Or we have to treat them as love would not wish to treat them? The answer is not to dilute our love with a little firmness and make a mixture, but to cling to both our love and our firmness.

A long time ago, I came across an expression which has helped me on this – stern love. Indulgent love says, "Do as you like." When you come to think about it, indulgent love is not love at all. Why is it that children nearly always prefer the teacher who is strict? There may be several reasons, but I'll tell you one: a strict teacher pays them a compliment – the compliment of saying to them,"You could be very good at this and I'm going to see that you become good at it." Whereas the indulgent person is saying in effect, "I don't mind how you turn out." God's love is stern, not indulgent.

Then there is care and trust. We take great care of our

children, rightly protecting them from danger – physical and moral. So what do we do when they want to climb a tree? Or ride a motorbike? Or go off on holiday with their friends. Again, compromise isn't the answer. We've got to find a way between the two.

Judy and I have learned one thing as parents. When children ask if they may do something, there are only two answers: either 'no' or 'yes, willingly'. The answer we are tempted to give, but which we should never give is,'yes, grudgingly'. "Well, yes, I suppose so. Your mother and I don't want you to do this at all. We think it is a bad idea, but if you must I suppose you'd better...." That takes all the fun out of it and they don't ask you any more.

Our son David announced three years ago that he was intending to bicycle to Athens. Judy and I gasped. Mind you, he was grown up and it would have been difficult to say no. Fortunately we didn't try. We said, "What a good idea! What a marvellous thing to do!" Well, then he knew he had our approval and support. So he could talk about it and he would even ask our advice. "Dad says I should wear a helmet."

Here is another: participation and perfection. We say to our children, "Come on, have a go. Never mind if it's not perfect." Then a little later we say, "You know, that wasn't good enough." They reply, 'But you said it didn't matter if it wasn't perfect." Both are right. In our desire to encourage participation we must not let them think that that 'near enough is good enough'.

Finally, what about prayer and work? We're told that things happen when we pray and that, if we don't pray, things don't happen. So, "Let's pray", we say, "and leave the rest." But things also happen when we make them happen. Well then, why pray? I can't tell you why but I do like the little saying, "You should pray as if there's no such thing as work and work as if there is no such thing as prayer." Charles Simeon, vicar of Holy Trinity Cambridge, in the 18th century, made a famous remark which really sums up all I am saying. "The truth," he said, "lies neither at one end nor the other, nor even in the middle, but at both ends at the same time."

"In the kingdom anything you want to keep, you've got to learn to give."

Sandy Millar *on some principles of giving*

One of the things that I think the church has to learn all over again is that it belongs to Jesus. We are Jesus's people. We were brought into existence for him. He is the head of the church. We are the body of the church. We are his body and we exist for him and not the other way round. We are intended to reflect him and his nature in the world. We are intended to be him and do the things that he does, to think the way he thinks.

For some of us, it's quite a shock because we've come from a world that's been teaching us exactly the opposite because the world has not been programmed by Jesus but by the enemies of Jesus. In Matthew 6:21, Jesus says one of the profoundest things we can ever hear: "For where your treasure is, there your heart will be also." There is a completely different sort of standard in the kingdom of God when we come from the dominion of darkness or the world.

The world has a number of preconceived axioms that we've been brought up on. One is that we are entitled to possessions, a certain degree of money, a certain degree of comfort, a certain degree of safety against the events of the world; so we have to make provision for ourselves and protect ourselves and get what we can. I'm not actually saying any of that is fatal, I'm just observing the principles.

So presumably if we're earning 'x' thousand a year and somebody offers us 'y' thousand a year, and 'y' is greater than 'x', it doesn't take us very long to think in terms of moving from x to y – what you get you keep. But what I want to observe is that when we come into the kingdom of God, a wholly different dynamic begins to operate. The dynamic in the kingdom of God is almost the exact opposite. It's what you give you keep. It's a giving mentality, a giving currency. It's so different from what, at one level, we hope to hear.

We have a feeling, somewhere at the back of our minds that anything we give, we've lost. I'm not just talking about money. In the kingdom, anything you want to keep, you've got to learn to give.

In Philippians 4:12, Paul says, "I have learnt …" In that context he's saying, "I have learnt how to have plenty of things and I have learnt how to have nothing." I think there is a wealth of experience behind that expression, "I have learnt." It wasn't easy. I don't think Paul was any happier to be poor than any of us but he learnt how to abound and how to be abased.

We have to learn to be in the giving economy. Somebody said to me again the other day, "I'm so lonely," and I said it almost without really thinking, "You know if you're lonely, you've got to give friendship." That's cruel, isn't it? No, it isn't. If you want love back, you've got to start learning to give it. I'm not saying you can do that overnight because many of us have been so battered by the world we don't know how to give anything except abuse.

But we come into the kingdom and suddenly discover that in the kingdom, there are people in the world who care about you. They seem to like you. They want to give things to you. They want to love you and pray for you, to sit up half the night ministering to you. It surprises you because you haven't seen that kind of thing outside the kingdom of God.

If you want friendship, you have to give it. If you want to keep your healing, you have to give it and pray for it. If you want salvation, you have to learn to give it. If you want to enjoy money, you have to learn to give it. This is the dynamic in the kingdom of God.

Let me attempt to persuade you in some other way. Do you know that every part of our service is designed around the concept that we come through those doors longing to give? In the old days we used to sing a big hymn of praise when we started. Why? Because the understanding is that we all come through the door so full of praise and love to God that we'd just burst if we were not given a chance to give him thanks and praise.

Somehow it got twisted along the way so that in many churches, you'll see the poor organist pumping away trying to get more volume, more steam, more excitement, more thrill, in order to get the congregation to sing more and get this hymn of praise out. That's what the Bible would call worship in the flesh. The Bible doesn't seem to think much of that.

Worship in the Spirit is when the congregation is so full of love, excitement and buzz, they come to church because it's the only building big enough for them all and they can't wait to sing their praises to God …. giving, giving. We give worship to God. In Matthew 6:4, Jesus says, "Then your Father, who sees what is done in secret, will reward you." What's the point of that? The point is that giving is done not primarily for anyone on this earth. Giving is primarily done for God.

I was asked to subscribe to something the other day. I couldn't because it was more money than I could have afforded to give and what was offered to me, done very nicely and very discreetly with beautiful print and glossy paper, was a chance to have my name included. But I don't want my name included here. I want my name included there, in heaven. The only way to get my name included there is if I don't get my name included here. I've got to make up my mind which I want because both are very tempting.

It's nice to feel that people think you're very generous, isn't it? But Jesus is saying that there is a reward in giving. In those days, word went out from the temple that they needed money and the trumpets would be blown and the messengers would go down the street. The godly man sitting in his stall in the bazaar somewhere, would put up the shutters and shut the door and hurry off to the temple. Everybody would nudge their neighbour and say, "You know where he's going? He's going to the temple because they've just sent a message saying they need money." Jesus was saying, "Don't do that. That's what the hypocrites do because they hope that you will have noticed."

From time to time, people ask me whether I teach on tithing. Tithing is a reference to the Old Testament where one of the offerings that the Jews were told to give was a tenth of their income as a free will offering. It was only one of the offerings they had to do. They had offerings for sin, offerings for the temple, offerings for the government, offerings for this and that.The free will offering was on top of that and it was a tenth.

I don't teach tithing because I think that in the Sermon on the Mount, Jesus is making a number of distinctions between the Old Testament emphasis which is on the activity, and the New Testament emphasis which is on the heart. I want us here to catch the New Testament spirit of giving.

The expression 'a tithe' or 'a tenth' is not a helpful one because the New Testament spirit of giving is that we give to God because he gave us everything. I cannot imagine God in heaven working out a tenth in order to give that to us, can you? I think he thought, "What can I give them? I'll give them my Son. I've only got one. I'll give them my Son. Jesus, would you go and get them, and rescue them and save them and die for them?"

Can you imagine Jesus saying, "What? Why should I go when I'm rich and I've got glory?" Can you see how foreign it is to the nature of God? Jesus didn't say that. Jesus said, "I'll go and Lord, how can we make it easier for them? I'll go simply and give up everything I've got." He who was rich became poor for our sakes, the New Testament tells us.

Paul says at the beginning of his letter to the Philippians that it was in response to that attitude that God said, "That is my man. I will now give him everything because he can be trusted." He was rich but he became poor.

In Matthew 6:19, Jesus goes on in that vein, "Don't store up treasures on earth, where moth and rust destroy, and where thieves break in and steal. But store up for yourselves treasures in heaven…"

William Law, commenting on that passage several hundred years ago, said it was as if a man had hands and eyes and feet which he could give to those who needed them, but instead of giving them to his blind or lame brethren, he locked them up in a chest. We would think he was rather selfish and inhuman, wouldn't we? But if he chose to amuse himself with hoarding them up rather than entitle himself to an eternal reward by giving them to those who needed them, might we not justly reckon him to be mad?

"A servant serves! That's how we know he is a servant."

Sandy Millar *on the importance of being servants*

One of the reasons that Paul's letter to the Ephesians is such an important part of the New Testament is that it speaks so much about God's intentions in bringing the church into existence, his love for the church, the grace that he has and continues to lavish upon her, the resources of his love and power that are available to her and – the bit we so often skip over in our excitement about the rest – his purposes for her here on earth.

> … for it is by grace you have been saved, through faith – and this is not from yourselves, it is the gift of God – not by works, so that no one can boast. For we are God's workmanship, created in Christ Jesus to do good works, which God prepared in advance for us to do. (Ephesians 2: 8-10)

I have often referred to the marks of the end-time church as generous, loving, obedient, worshipping – GLOW.

Obedience means doing what God tells us to do. It doesn't mean delegating what God's told us to do to someone else. Nor does it mean reverently explaining to God why what he has told us to do is impractical, impossible or more likely ought to wait for a more suitable time! We have been ".. created to do good works." I want to suggest that in practice, if we are to fulfil our calling in this way, we shall have to keep constantly under review two areas of our lives.

Our attitude. Paul writes to the Philippian church:

> "Your attitude should be the same as that of Christ Jesus who being in very nature God… made himself nothing taking the very nature of a servant, being made in human likeness… He humbled himself and became obedient to death…" (Philippians 2:5-8).

The Christian calling is to serve, to be obedient, to do good works, and to see that not as part of the rather unpleasant aspects of struggling along but as the highest possible calling, with rewards of their own on earth as well as later in heaven. That is why the world has never had any time for the true Christian attitude (but admires it deeply when it sees it) for the world recognises only power that seeks to rule. Jesus and his followers exercise a power that seeks to serve and such power is misnamed 'weakness' by the world.

It is obvious in public life that with the diminishing

influence of the Christian faith, the desire to serve has been correspondingly lost and the desire to rule, which is always at the heart of unredeemed human affairs, has correspondingly emerged more obviously. Paradoxically, as the desire to rule has become more obvious, so has the influence of those in public life diminished.

More seriously, the same worldly attitude is becoming more deeply embedded in the heart of the church and unless we see what is happening and turn from it, we shall not be able or willing to fulfil this high purpose for which God has called us.

Do we see ourselves as servants, ready to do what God tells us? In the words of the old prayer, 'to spend and be spent' in God's service, to him and to others? Narrowing it down perhaps more uncomfortably – do we see our education, training, 'social skills', position, possessions and money as qualifying us to rule, as the world does, or as having been given to us in order to serve as Christ does and did?

Human nature has always been the same. You may remember when Solomon died, his son Rehoboam became king. The Israelites got up a petition and sent Jeroboam (one of Solomon's officials who had had to flee when Solomon tried to kill him) to ask on behalf of all the Israelites if they could look forward to an easier life under the new king, in return for which they promised to be loyal to him and to serve him.

Rehoboam very sensibly consulted his father's advisers who told him: "If today you will be a servant to these people and serve them and give them a favourable answer, they will always by your servants." But their advice was unacceptable to Rehoboam, presumably because he thought it was inconsistent to be a king and a servant. As a result he was overthrown and the kingdom was divided. (1 Kings 12)

Jesus, by contrast, was a king who came to serve and his followers, who share some aspects of his kingship, can most obviously be seen to be his followers by their willingness to serve. That too was the message of what must have been an incredibly embarrassing incident for them, when James and John came to Jesus and asked to be given the seats of honour on his left and right when he came in his glory (Mark 10).

It provoked such trouble amongst the disciples that Jesus got them together to sort it out and teach them the lesson that each generation has to learn for themselves:

> You know that those who are regarded as rulers of the Gentiles lord it over them and their high officials exercise authority over them. Not so with you. Instead, whoever wants to become great among you must be a servant, and whoever wants to be first must be slave of all. For even the Son of Man did not come to be served, but to serve and to give his life as a ransom for many (Mark 10: 42-45).

Activity. A servant serves! That's how we know he is a servant. Good works will include things we do for God inside and outside the context of the church building. A church like ours can only function because people come with the desire to do something – anything – and allow God to tell them what it might be, visible or not very visible, apparently important or very humble. The ideal servant sees or hears what needs to be done, and does it! If we want to catch the attention of the world for Jesus, and we do, it will be through not just what we say but what we do and how we do it.

I appeal to you to join me in reviewing honestly, on your own with God and with your family – if you have one – your own priorities and attitudes and activities, not as an exercise in guilt but as a means of fulfilling the call that God has on your life. I can't think of a more important issue for us as a church today or a more fulfilling one.

One final word: Paul's opening words to the Ephesians are a reminder to them of who they are in Christ, and of their importance to God and the place they have in his heart. The test of spiritual maturity is not the ability to speak in tongues, prophesy, memorise or expound Scripture. It is the ability and willingness to serve God and others through good works, learning to love the unlovely and serve them, to value those whom the world has discarded.

But Paul's point is this: it is only as we know who we are in Christ and all the resources of heaven that are ours, that we shall have the power, love and victory that is needed to serve and change the lives of those whom, for God and with God, we are seeking to serve.

"Commitment is not a dirty word, is it? It's actually a wonderfully secure word."

Sandy Millar *on commitment*

Then Joshua assembled all the tribes of Israel at Shechem. He summoned the elders, leaders, judges and officials of Israel, and they presented themselves before God. (Joshua 24:1)

I'd love to feel that is what we are doing. We've allowed the Spirit of God to speak to us, to encourage us, to touch us, to communicate with us – as we present ourselves before God. Then we come to the verse where God calls his people through Joshua to what we would call commitment. Joshua said to the people:

This is what the Lord, the God of Israel, says...Now fear the Lord and serve him with all faithfulness. Throw away the gods your forefathers worshipped beyond the River and in Egypt, and serve the Lord. But if serving the Lord seems undesirable to you, then choose for yourselves this day whom you will serve, whether the gods your forefathers served beyond the River, or the gods of the Amorites, in whose land you are living. But as for me and my household, we will serve the Lord. (Joshua 24:14-15)

Commitment is not a dirty word, is it? It's actually a wonderfully secure word. We get a hint of that in that it is so rarely valued in our present culture. The people said to Joshua, "We will serve the Lord our God and obey him," and he made a covenant for the people.

I want to earth this into our activities – a commitment to Christ, a commitment to live as disciples of Christ and to be of use to the world where we are, whether as Christian bus drivers, bankers, dustmen, doctors, lawyers, professional people, unprofessional people. We want to bring back into equality of recognition within the kingdom of God, that every job and every person doing a job has a value. We pledge ourselves to build up the local Christian community and make it as near to heaven as we can.

We commit ourselves to love one another, to have unity with one another and to plant churches. Then there is a commitment to resourcing the vision – such a thrilling vision. It's a much bigger vision than any one of us but the issue which faces us, faced Joshua's people. We can't do it on our own. The question is: are we ready for the cost?

Let me suggest a couple of challenges to our faith and commitment: firstly it seems to me just conceivably possible that, in the interest of a home group or church plant, you may be asked by the Lord to move job or house and secondly, you may have to risk looking foolish. That's what the writer to Hebrews said: 'scorning the shame'. The shame of the cross. I've often thought the most agonising aspect of Jesus on the cross was seeing his mother, and the disappointment that he wasn't able to explain to her and help her to see why it was necessary that her son should die on the cross. We may have to scorn shame.

We have to resist contemporary culture. We have to go for a Christian view of sex. The ingenuity with which the world at the moment – the unbelievers, the liberal elements in the church – are attempting to redraft the Christian manifesto is breathtaking because they want to look like Christians but not bear the shame of the cross. We want a community that is worth planting. A community that is going to have purity in relationships and love. A community that is able to have relationships in an uncluttered way, free from innuendo, suggestion, any hint of impropriety.

It isn't 'cool', I am told, to want purity in relationships – but morality is of vital importance. Purity in relationships is important. God hates divorce – hates it. If you're divorced, God bless you. We want to be sympathetic and minister and to do everything that we can to help, but I am only saying what you want me to say. I've spoken to many people who have been through divorces. It's the most agonising thing and we have to say, "God hates it." That's what the Bible tells us. It's not a Christian option.

We may just have to risk the shame in countering too the modern cultural attitude towards children. Children in the Bible are a tremendous blessing. They are hard work but they are worth every ounce of that hard work. There is no higher calling recognised by God than the patient, loving, caring, home-bound attitude towards bringing up children.

Mothers, if you have children that you're bringing up, you are fulfilling in that job alone your ministry to the church. Husbands, your primary ministry is to your wife. Wives, your primary ministry is to your husband and family – and children are the key in that. The pressure from the modern culture is: "When are you coming back to work Jean?" "Oh, I'm not." "Not? What you going to do? Look after babies all day?" "Yes, my babies and I'm going to bring them up and pray for them and teach them."

Thirdly, we risk 'not looking cool' in our attitude to giving, but this needs resourcing. I'm not talking about everyday giving. We're all called to give to the church but there will be some people whose ministry to the church is giving.

Everyone gets a prize as they come into line with Jesus Christ. "May our attitude be that of Christ, who being in himself God, counted not equality with God as something to be grasped..." What is it going to cost you? I know that it cost him everything.

"The 'New Morality' is the old immorality by another name."

Sandy Millar *on how sex can be enjoyed to the full – God's perfect way*

The secular world has changed since I was at school. It's been a process, a steady drip feed of poison. It's in the culture – in the literature, the books, the films, the television programmes, the magazines – because steadily, over that period of 30 years we've been living off and steadily running out of Christian capital. So those things which when I was at school, I would have had to make a furtive and serious expedition to the centre of Soho to find, are now in most newsagents and outside on the pavement. Whether it's hard porn, soft porn or just offensive and indecent, the Bible knows no distinction. They are man-made, secular distinctions in order to justify a trend.

The point is that they know where we are weakest and you and I are being manipulated by commercial interests fed by the devil himself, whose main interest is in separating us from God. Over those 30 years or so, they have steadily moved the goalposts so that what is acceptable now to talk about, to look at and to do would have been unthinkable at that time.

That is one aspect of the issue, but that attitude is creeping into the church, where it never used to be and there's confusion, hurt and damage being done to people we don't want to damage, to hurt and to see confused.

So the overall question is, "I am a Christian. What do I do about sex?" I want to look at Genesis 2 because sex after all was God's invention. You'd really think nowadays that it was an invention of the world's and that God was looking down from heaven, thinking, "Oh my goodness, whatever will they think of next?" He actually thought of sex before we were born. He must have done, mustn't he!

Here's the Christian doctrine of marriage:

> For this reason a man will leave his father and mother and be united to his wife and they will become one flesh. The man and his wife were both naked, and they felt no shame. (Genesis 2: 24-25)

The Christian doctrine of marriage is the most exciting, thrilling and positive doctrine that there is in the Bible, because what it sets before us is God's perfect plan. That doesn't mean that if you're not married, you're not part of God's perfect plan – you are. But his doctrine so far as sex is concerned, is contained in his doctrine of marriage which is that in the ideal world, a man will leave a perfect happy family; his fiancee will leave her perfect happy family and they will be joined together by God and from that union, they will be united and become one flesh.

On the day Annette and I got married we went into the church at Stoke Poges with two heads, two bodies and, notionally speaking, the Bible describes that we came out with one head and one body. We were united. We hadn't become one flesh up until then but we were united. Springing from that unity, enhancing that unity, recreating and reminding us of that unity, we came together physically in sex which was the consummation and the completion of the marriage.

Now Paul says – and you can't get a higher doctrine than this

– that the relationship between a husband and a wife is the nearest thing you can get on earth to the relationship that exists between Christ and the church. There is a unity between Christ and the church which is indivisible, inseparable – a total unity. The unity between a husband and a wife reflects that spiritual unity between Christ and the church.

In due course, through the physical union of the man and the wife which comes after the pre-existent spiritual union, a child is born and he is the perfect evidence of the pre-existent unity, both physical obviously, but equally importantly spiritual unity of his parents. As you know, people spend hours trying to work out if he is like his daddy or his mummy; the fact is that he's like both of them. Why? Because God ordained it that way. That's why it is such a devastating thing for a child if his parents come unstuck because subconsciously, it puts a question mark, a threat over his or her very existence until he or she re-finds their existence again in Jesus Christ and the Spirit of God ministers to them.

It is for that reason that it is not possible to have a physical sexual relationship which does not affect you spiritually. It's bound to, indeed it was intended to. In 1 Corinthians 6, Paul writes:

The body is not meant for sexual immorality, but for the Lord, and the Lord for the body. By his power God raised the Lord from the dead, and he will raise us also. Do you not know that your bodies are members of Christ himself? Shall I then take the members of Christ and unite them with a prostitute? Never! Do you not know that he who unites himself with a prostitute is one with her in body? For it is said: 'the two will become one flesh'. But he who unites himself with the Lord is one with him in spirit. Flee from sexual immorality. All other sins a man commits are outside his body, but he who sins sexually sins against his own body. Do you not know that your body is a temple of the Holy Spirit, who is in you, whom you have received from God? You are not your own; you were bought at a price. Therefore honour God with your body. (1 Cor 6:13-20)

What Paul is saying of course is that sex is not a casual thing. It matters who you sleep with. It affects you because in the giving of yourself in sex, you cannot give yourself to A on one day, to B on another day, to C on another day – however far apart A, B, or C may be spaced – and then tear yourself away from A and give yourself entirely to B and tear yourself away from B and give yourself entirely to C, without being affected by it.

So God's idea in sex is that it is the fulfilment of a unity for life that he has created, reflecting the unity between Christ and you. As with everything God is involved in, it is a creative union. The Bible is against everything else because the Bible is for sex in marriage. Anything else is a corruption or a perversion at worst of what God has created as the perfect relationship for his people.

Homosexual practising relationships are sterile, uncreative and not of God. Masturbation is solo, getting rather than giving – not of God. Fornication between unmarried people is coming together without commitment for life – not of God. There is no total, complete giving of oneself in fornication.

But what if you say to me, "I am a girl in this fellowship and I've met this guy; he really loves me and I really love him. We are totally committed to each other. What about that – can we sleep together?" The only way of total commitment is to get married. Why don't you get married? If you're not ready to be totally sure, don't sleep together. God is calling into existence a people who are, intend and want to be holy. That's what is going on. That is why there is such attack about it.

Don't be conned by this 'New Morality'. There is nothing new about the so-called 'New Morality'. Sometimes younger people suggest that the biblical view seems out of touch and old-fashioned. If I may say so, if you have fallen for the 'New Morality', it's you that's old fashioned. Because the 'New Morality' is the old immorality by another name. The people of God were always tempted to pervert God's will, and immorality and godlessness have always gone together. So it's no coincidence that with the lessening of the impact of the Christian faith over the last 25-30 years, and the growth of a rather arrogant paganism that seems to think it can exist without God's love, protection, power and grace, the brazenness of the new immorality has increased.

Is purity possible? In Hebrews 12:14, the author says, "Make every effort to live in peace with all men and to be holy; without holiness no-one will see the Lord." The author is determined that we are to be holy because if we're not holy, we won't see God. It makes sense. Heaven wouldn't be heaven if we got there in the state most of us were in before we were saved. The justification, the saving of us, is in order to set us apart from that stuff and bring us into the sanctity of a family in which these things are unthinkable.

Holiness is a process. It consists of steps in the right direction. Every time we say yes to the Spirit of God, every time we say no to the enemy, we have made another step in the right direction and we will wake up one day and find that our transformation is complete by the Spirit of God. It's not complete yet, but – God willing – one day it will be. So it is possible.

The $64,000 question: how do I stay pure? How are we to achieve this standard? Firstly, be honest. I think we would admit that most of our dealings with God never took on a reality until we were honest with him. Jacob had to go through that; we have to go through that. Admit where we're weak, admit where we're sinful and repent.

I remember John Collins, my predecessor, saying that if you're a burglar, you don't gradually give up burgling when you come to Christ. You stop NOW – no more burgling. I remember watching this rather cultured congregation and I could see straight away the resolve on the faces of each one of them: 'No more burgling'. But it hasn't got to be burgling. It is repenting of anything which is spoiling our life. Turn from it. Throw away those magazines. Stop taking the paper if it means you have to go and collect it and look at those magazines every time. Stop it or it will destroy you.

Temptations go on and on. You people who are unmarried think that we who are married are never tempted and ought not to be. I quite agree. But we are, so whatever it is that is causing trouble, STOP IT! Deal with it just as you would if someone offered you poison with a label on it because of course the enemy never shows you a picture of what you will be if you consistently give in to that temptation.

Secondly, marry! Paul says it's much better. For some of us, it is inconceivable that we could go through life unmarried. Well, then marry. Some of you – I am talking to men now – are in a position to marry; you're quite well off, you can afford it. Think about it. I'm not one to speak because I took seven years to propose to my wife. If you are married, cultivate faithfulness within marriage and chuck out everything within your marriage that springs more from lust than from love. Why do you think the author to the Hebrews says that marriage should be held honourable by all and 'the marriage bed undefiled'. What do you think he means by that? How do you defile a marriage bed? By bringing into it lust.

I was talking to a couple the other day who have a tremendous ministry in deliverance. He said something to me that I found surprising. "Many of the people I've ministered to recently", he said, "have got into spiritual oppression through oral sex, even in marriage." It's unproductive, it's uncreative so chuck it! Stop it, in or out of marriage.

So, fellers, marry or put sex out of your minds. Now I recognise that in saying that, it's hard on those who are longing to get married. So, thirdly, if you are not married and not in a position to get married, Paul suggests that in some ways you may be better off.

I want to tell you of St Augustine's confessions. He was in absolute agonies because he was a sensual man; he lived with a girl who was below him in his social station – which is what prevented him from marrying her – and he couldn't see how he could ever live a holy life. He said; "For I felt my past to have a grip on me. It uttered wretched cries: How long? How long is it to be? Tomorrow, tomorrow." "But why not now?" I said. "Why not an end to my impure life in this very hour?"

He was in a bitter agony, weeping and crying out to God because he knew there was something better but he'd never found it. Then he heard the voice of a boy or girl – he doesn't know which it was – in the next door garden. They were playing a game of some kind which involved saying, "Pick it up and read, pick it up and read."

These are his words:

At once my countenance changed and I began to think intently whether there might be some sort of children's game in which such a chant is used, but I couldn't remember having heard of one. I checked the flood of tears and stood up. I interpreted it solely as a divine command to me to open the book and read the first chapter I might find... So I hurried back to the place where...I'd put the book of the apostle when I'd got up. I seized it, opened it and in silence I read the first passage on which my eyes lit: "Not in riots and drunken parties; not in eroticism and indecencies; not in strife and rivalry; but put on the Lord Jesus Christ and make no provision for the flesh in its lusts." [Romans 13:13-14] I neither wished nor needed to read further. At once, with the last words of this sentence, it was as if a light of relief from all anxiety flooded into my heart. All the shadows of doubt were dispelled. The effect of your converting me to yourself was that I did not now seek a wife and had no ambition for success in this world.

Augustine began on the course of life which led to us now calling him Saint Augustine. He was no saint before that. After he'd lived with a girl for 12 or 13 years, as he had, he didn't say, "Oh it's hard." He said, "Oh God, I've found something better." By God's grace.

"There we are at the bottom of the ocean going: 'Bubble, bubble, glug, glug.'"

David Parker *on a dependent relationship with God*

I think of so many things in terms of pictures and my picture of what our life is like from the fall onwards, is a parable of deep sea diving. You and I were created underwater – at the bottom of the ocean. We all had lifelines to the surface where we could breathe air. There we were in the garden, all walking around on the bottom of the ocean saying, "This is good" and the presence of the Lord was there. But we decided it was a little encumbering to be hooked up to this lifeline. Wouldn't it be better to cut it off and just go on our own? So we rejected God's provision and we rejected relationship with him. We cut ourselves off through sin and the fall.

There we are at the bottom of the ocean going, "Bubble, bubble, glug, glug." But God told us, "If you do this, you will surely die." So the only question that remains now is, how long can you hold your breath? Some people, amazingly, can hold their breath for 80 or 90 years. They just hold their breath, never acknowledging that they were made dependent on God. You and I were made, as Jesus said, to live by every word that comes out of the mouth of God. We were not made independent. We derive our life from our connection, our relationship with God. He sent his Son through the surface of the waters to the very bottom of the ocean, to reconnect us with the lifeline and it cost the Son his life to do that. He came to reconnect you to the surface, to bring back the breath of God into your life.

"The choice is between life ... and death."

David Parker *on a matter of life and death*

For some time, I found myself making these excruciating decisions to do what God wanted, instead of what I wanted and I thought of myself as so heroic. Then, one day the Lord graciously came to me and said, "Son, you think the choice is between life on my terms and life on your terms." I said, "Yes. That's it, Lord. That's the choice I've got." He said, "That's not the choice. The choice is between life ... and death."

Prayer

"I start by going out into the garden – if it's not raining – and singing a loud song of praise."

Bishop Lesslie Newbigin *on personal prayer*

We will not learn to pray without ceasing unless we also set aside times which are particularly for prayer, when our whole attention is focused on prayer and on nothing else. Now there are many guidebooks about how one should spend these times and I suppose that everybody in the end has to find his or her own way. I think we ought to be growing in our prayer life. We ought to be reviewing our practice and seeing whether we are becoming stale, or are in a rut, but I will simply tell you what I do. I don't think that I am a model but it's useful to say something. I am sure there are many people who are far ahead of me in these matters.

I make sure that I have a clear half hour before breakfast, absolutely undisturbed. I start by going out into the garden – if it's not raining – and singing a loud song of praise. It was the great William Laud in his book about a devout and holy life, who said you should always begin by singing a hymn of praise (not just thinking it or mumbling it but singing it) and anyone who has heard my voice will understand why I go into the garden if I can. Then I think about those acts of God which especially concern that day.

Sunday: the creation of light, the separation of light from darkness, and all that it means; the resurrection of Jesus on the first day and the gift of the Spirit on the first day. Sunday is a very rich day for the first part of my prayers.

Monday: the creation of the firmament, the rain, the snow, the clouds, the mist; all the mysterious powers, the invisible powers which exist, although it's hard for us to visualise them; the unseen realities which we can only dimly grasp but which we know are God's servants and obey his command.

Tuesday: the day he separated the water from the land. I think about the dry land, the rocks that underlie it, the soil that covers it, the ploughed fields, the meadows, the trees, the mountains, the trees and the flowers and the grass, and all the particular bits of the world that I love very specially and I thank God for them.

Wednesday: the creation of the sun and the moon and the stars, and therefore the times and seasons; the rich variety that we have as we move from winter into spring, into summer then autumn, and back into winter – all the joy that we get from the varying of the seasons.

Thursday: the fishes and the birds, and all their magnificent multitude; and of course, the ascension of Jesus on that Thursday and his seating at the right hand of the Father, reigning with the Father over all things.

Friday: the cross; the creation of the human family; the fall and the story of God's patient dealing with his erring family, leading up to the cross and the passion of Jesus.

Saturday: that mysterious day when Jesus lies in the tomb and when we remember those who have fallen asleep in Christ. It is a time when I specially remember my own parents and all who have been very dear to me, who have died. I remember them name by name, and I thank God for them. And so we come again to Sunday.

This gives one a distinct subject matter for praise at the beginning of the morning's prayer. Then I read a psalm, an Old Testament passage and a New Testament passage, and I try to place each passage within the whole context of God's story of creation and redemption.

After this I say the Lord's prayer – often saying it two or three times over because every phrase in it needs to be said with all one's heart and mind. Then I say the collect of the day, I take out my diary and I look at the day's agenda – at the things that are coming up, the people I am going to meet, the crises that may come, the decisions that have to be made – and I pray for God's grace for that day.

Then I turn to intercession. Our intercessory prayer needs to be serious. Everyone makes their own arrangements. I have three 'schedules': those things and people for whom I pray every day; those for whom I pray weekly; those for whom I pray monthly. You cannot hold more than a certain amount in one time of prayer.

My wife and I always have our evening prayer together in which we read a portion of the New Testament, thank God for the day, ask forgiveness for our sin, lay before God any very special concerns, and pray for our family. We finish with a prayer for the night. That is my particular pattern of prayer at this point in my journey.

"Go on faithfully, even if it seems as dry as dust."

Bishop Lesslie Newbigin *on praying through dry times*

What about those periods when everything is dry? There are days, thank God, when our hearts are deeply touched and we feel it's all so real that we want to run out and shout to the world, "This is the reality." But there are other days when the same words seem to mean almost nothing. What do we do about that?

Well, the first thing is to remember that all serious praying people know that experience. God gives us times of comfort and joy and he gives us times of darkness when only faith can hold us on. But that is part of his training – that we learn to walk even when we cannot see.

For me, the great model is something that I've learned from climbing in the Alps. You set out on a wonderful morning and against the blue sky, there is the white peak of the mountain you're setting out to climb. You go up and up and then you come into the mist and you can see nothing. Everything is blotted out. The one thing that you have is the track and you can go on putting one foot in front of the other on it, trusting that the track is reliable. Thank God, in Switzerland they generally are! Eventually, you come out and see the mountain again.

That's the model for our periods of darkness and dryness. Keep to your discipline of prayer. Go on faithfully even if it seems as dry as dust. Because God, who knows what he's doing and doesn't fool around with us, is teaching us what we need. He gives us everything we need to learn to walk by faith and not by sight. So, above all, don't give up your regular discipline of prayer but know that God is leading you in his own way.

"I think that the whole Bible teaches us that God does... change his mind."

Bishop Lesslie Newbigin *on intercession*

Intercession is something about which people have puzzled. If God knows already what we need and what we want, what is the good of it? He knows best. There is a phrase that William

Temple used which I have come to question. He said that the idea that we pray in order to change God's mind would be an enterprise blasphemous in the attempt and calamitous in the accomplishment.

Well yes, in a sense. But that sounds a little like the thought that God is a kind of implacable, immovable, unshakeable power to which we simply have to submit, and why bother him with our ideas when he will do what he knows best in the end. That is much more like a Moslem concept of prayer than a Christian concept.

Jesus lays tremendous stress upon intercessory, petitionary prayer – battering at the gates of God's house to ask him for what we need. One cannot escape from that – it is so central in Jesus's teaching. I think that the whole Bible teaches us that God does, if you like, change his mind. Over and over again, there is the story of stubborn rebellion and then repentance. Repentance – honest returning to God – does lead him to turn to us.

The relationship that God has with us, however hard it may be for us to understand it metaphysically, certainly in the context of the Bible and of all Jesus's teaching, is such that God desires our prayer because it is precisely in our praying that we are brought more fully into the mind of God.

I think that we have to take as our model, as so often, the prayer of Jesus in Gethsemane. That prayer has two parts.

The first part is, "If it be thy will, let this cup pass from me." Jesus prays to be delivered from the appalling agony and dereliction of the cross. Then the second part, "Nevertheless, not my will, but thine be done." Now I don't think we should use the second part simply to obliterate the first part. I think both parts are an essential part of our praying – that God wants us to bring our desires, our needs, our longings to him. And that has one important consequence – it means that we should be serious in our praying.

I have, for a long time, made it a custom that when I

undertake to pray for some particular outcome, group or person, I write this down and I go on praying until I know, or hope I know, how God has answered that prayer. There is a tick and that becomes an item for thanksgiving. Surely it would not be taking God seriously if we simply tossed off a petition and then forgot that we had asked it, so that we were not ready to listen for God's answer?

"It's all part of our training."

Bishop Lesslie Newbigin *on wandering thoughts in prayer*

You can't talk about prayer without talking about wandering thoughts. You set out to pray and suddenly wake up to find you're thinking about something quite different. Everybody has that problem. What do you do about it? I think the answer is quite simple – you pray for the thing or person that you were wanderingly thinking about and then you quietly come back to your prayers.

Don't worry. Everybody has that problem. Just raise up that person or situation and ask God for what is appropriate. Then return to the central line of your prayers. And even if you have to do that 10 or 20 times during your prayers, don't worry. It's all part of our training.

"The battle was not decided on the battlefield. The battle was decided on the praying field."

Pastor David Yonggi Cho *on praying for victory*

Korean people love Great Britain because the first missionary to Korea was from Great Britain. His name was Reverend Thomas. As soon as he arrived 120 years ago, he was executed by the Korean government. The blood of his martrydom cried to the throne of God and, as a result, now more than thirty percent of the population is Christian. Whenever we think of Great Britain, we think of Reverend Thomas who died for the salvation of Korea. The Bible says, "Cast your breath into the water and lo, afterwards you shall regain." So he cast his breath into the Korean water and, as the breath, I am returning to Great Britain to become a blessing to you.

I am deeply moved in my Spirit because I am already seeing revival here. I think the presence of the kingdom of God is so powerful in this place. You are a holy nation. Here is a scripture reading from Exodus 17:8-13.

The Amalekites came and attacked the Israelites at Rephidim. Moses said to Joshua, 'Choose some of our men and go out to fight the Amalekites. Tomorrow I will stand on top of the hill with the staff of God in my hands.' So Joshua fought the Amalekites as Moses had ordered, and Moses, Aaron and Hur went to the top of the hill. As long as Moses held up his hands, the Israelites were winning, but whenever he lowered his hands the Amalekites were winning. When Moses' hands grew tired, they took a stone and put it under him and he sat on it. Aaron and Hur held his hands up – one on one side, one on the other – so that his hands remained steady till sunset. So Joshua overcame the Amalekite army with the sword.

The Amalekites were so powerful. The Israelites were losing the battle. It was a desperate situation. Moses was on top of the hill, giving up intercessory prayer for Joshua and his army in the battlefield. Then they prevailed over the Amalekites. When Moses got tired, put his arms down and stopped intercessory prayer, then the power stopped flowing and the Amalekites got stronger. But Moses continued intercessory prayer until the going down of the sun. Joshua was enabled to smite the Amalekites completely and they had a tremendous victory that day.

We can see from this story that the battle was not decided on the battlefield. The battle was decided on the praying field. Many people think that the battle is being fought on the battlefield and that victory or defeat will be decided there. But as we see, the decisive battle was fought on the hill through intercessory prayer.

Christians are out there in the battleground and politicians also. People are fighting every day in the battlefield. Sin, corruption, hatred, unrighteousness, filthiness, sickness, disease, obsession, possession, oppression, depression, failure, hunger, curse, death and hell are all out to attack people, to destroy churches, to destroy the Christians, to destroy society.

We can't just stand back and criticise. By criticising we can't accomplish anything. We are fighting a losing battle. Who can relieve us from this predicament? Can education prevail against sin? Can politics prevail against this enemy? Could revolution/evolution of the society prevail against this enemy? Throughout human history, we tried everything but we found that we were lacking power. The Amalekites have been victorious in every place. But now God is raising 20th century Moseses. You are in the place of Moses, Aaron and Hur.

We have come together to carry out intercessory prayer for

the church of Great Britain, for the politicians, for the civilians, for the British people. We have not gathered together to pass criticism. We are here to pray for the nation and to release the power of God for this nation. Politicians can't solve the problem. Science can't solve the problem. Only the power of God can overcome this enemy.

My Bible says God never changes. My Bible says Jesus is the same yesterday, today and forever. We see the sin. We see the suffering. We see the corruption. We see the poverty but the power of God is only to be released when the Christian church comes together and prays. When you pray, God releases power but when you stop praying, God's power stops. God is omnipotent, omniscient and omnipresent but still God works through your prayers. You say, "God can perform a miracle without me," but that's your idea not God's idea. We are working together to bring this nation back to the Heavenly Father. To carry out a very effective intercessory prayer we must prepare our lives.

Firstly, our intercessory prayer should be **founded on the redemption of our Lord Jesus Christ.** We must stand upon the blood of Jesus Christ to enter the presence of God. Without the blood, we wouldn't have any access to the throne of God. His blood still prevails, still speaks, so when we carry out intercessory prayer we must know that the blood of Jesus Christ purchased us from sin. The blood of Jesus Christ reconciled us to the Heavenly Father so that we might have the love of God and the sanctification of God. The blood of Jesus Christ purchased us spirit, soul and body.

My Bible says Christ has redeemed us from the curse of the Law, so that the blessing of Abraham might come upon the Gentiles. Through the blood of Jesus, God destroyed death and hell. So when we stand on the blood, no enemy can stand against us. When we carry out intercessory prayer, we must not forget that we should pray through the blood of Jesus Christ.

Secondly, when we want to carry out victorious intercessory

prayer **we must repent of all the sins in our lives.** If we hide our sin, God cannot listen to us. One of our sisters in the church came to be healed from a facial paralysis and I prayed for her many times but nothing ever happened. She went to the hospital and received treatment but was not healed. She went to the Chinese doctors and received acupuncture but nothing happened. Finally, she became very discouraged. She came to my office and she was crying. And I lost my confidence because I had prayed for her many times and she was not healed.

Then after a while, I was praying and the Spirit spoke into my heart, "I can't heal her while she keeps enmity in her spirit." So I said, "Sister, do you hate anybody?" She said, "Yes, my in-laws. I hate my father-in-law, my mother-in-law, my brother-in-law and sister-in-law. I work like a horse in their house but they don't appreciate me. They always criticise me. There is bitterness in my soul." I said that if there was bitterness in her soul, then God could not heal her. She was crying. She said, "I can't love them. If you were in my position, you would know my situation. I can't love them."

Then, I was listening to the voice of the Holy Spirit. He said to me, "Don't force her to love. Just ask her to forgive. After forgiving them, if there is some power left over, then start to love." So I told her this. She nodded her head and said that she could forgive them. So we called each of the members of her family's name to forgive them. Then she said, "I have forgiven them all. Will you pray for me?" I laid my hands upon her and I was praying, and out of curiosity I peeped open my eyes to see. I was amazed because right in front of my eyes, her paralysis was disappearing and she was getting healed. I experienced the power of the forgiveness. God never sees the outside of you. He looks inside you. Once you hide sin in your heart, he won't listen to your prayer.

So when praying, we must confess all the known sin in our lives. We should confess unrighteousness, our hatred, our faithlessness, our pride, our inhumility. We should cleanse our lives from these things. Then God will hear our prayer.

Thirdly, **you have to depend on the Holy Spirit.** Say to him, "We do not know how to pray but you are here to help me so, help me to pray, Holy Spirit. I recognise you. I depend upon you." Then the Spirit will intervene and will help you to carry out victorious intercessory prayer. When you pray, God intervenes so ask the Holy Spirit to help. He's here to help you. God is on the throne. Jesus Christ is seated at his right hand but the Spirit of God is here on earth. He is working together with you.

Fourthly, **you must study the Bible.** You must stand on the word of God. The heavens shall pass away but the word of God shall never pass away. Ask the Holy Spirit to teach you the word of God. When you stand on the word of God and you carry out intercessory prayer then your prayer will be riding the power.

When you pray, the devil will come and put all kinds of hindrances on to you. You will see so many impossible things happen in your lives. When you stand upon the Word, then whether you can see, hear or feel, you will not be swayed by the situation and circumstances. Then you can prevail and carry out victorious intercessory prayer.

Fifthly, when you pray, **you must pray for the glory of God.** If we have any ulterior motive in our hearts then God won't listen. Whatever we do, we should do for the glory of God. We have all gathered together to see the glory of God and so God is ready to accept our prayers because we are praying for the glory of God. And that is very necessary.

The real fight is going on in your intercessory prayer. The devil will bring all kind of hindrances to the praying people or church. He won't let you study the Bible. He won't let you in the fellowship. He will try to stop you praying because the battle is won at the prayer meeting. Many look at the TV and read newspapers. You see that very important issues are being discussed in the political circle. And you will say, "I'm power-less." Prayer is the answer for this nation. Prayer is the answer for your problem. Prayer is the answer for your business.

Once when Billy Graham visited Korea I asked him, "If you wanted to leave a word to Christian people in the world before you die, what word would you like to leave?" He looked at me, smiled and said, "Brother Cho, I would say to the Christians of the world – number one, pray; number two, pray; number three, pray."

I already see revival here. I already see the power of prayer in your lives. You are the answer to this nation. You are the catalyst of a great revival in this nation. And so let us make this a turning point in the history of Great Britain. God will give a decisive victory over the Amalekites in your country because you are here on the hill, in the place of Moses, Aaron and Hur. And since you have prayed, there will be victory after victory.

"I think my Christian life has gained so much more from being part of this."

Glenda Waddell *on intercession*

I had felt uncomfortable for quite a while about the fact that I wasn't interceding. I didn't regard myself as an intercessory sort of person. I was much more a receiving sort of person. I was quite good at praising and reading the Bible, and generally letting God minister to me. I was quite scathing of people who went to God with long shopping lists. I didn't think it was for me.

Then I sat through a service at the end of which Jeremy

Jennings, Pastoral Director of Holy Trinity Brompton, asked people to stand and commit themselves to intercede. As the service had gone on, I had felt more and more uncomfortable and thought I heard God saying, "I've given you so much. Won't you do this thing for me?"

All the time, another voice was saying, "You couldn't do that. You'd never keep it up. It would be doomed to failure from the beginning. You're not the intercessory type. Let someone else do it who's got more time." At that time, I think I was probably busier than I'd ever been in my life. I was under more stress than I'd ever been and I was really tired. I couldn't believe that God would ask me to do this. But in the end, I did stand and I said, "Lord if you really want me to do this, will you wake me?"

I went to bed and I set the alarm, fully expecting to sleep through it as I had been doing. To my horror, I found myself sitting bolt upright the next morning at 5am! I said, "Oh no! I really can't face this!" Anyway, I went downstairs, sat in a chair with a cup of coffee and said, "Lord, I honestly don't know what to do. I don't know what intercession is. I don't know how you do intercession but if you want me to do it, I'll do it."

I sat there for a bit and then I think I started to pray in tongues. Almost immediately I had two pictures. One was of a dove flying and carrying what seemed to be a message. I understood that to mean that the prayers were being carried to the throne room. The other one was of a huge mountain made of wax – there was a light on a candle set into the mountain. I got the words from Psalm 97 that in the presence of the Lord, the mountains melt like wax. God said, "This is intercession. Go for it."

So I started to pray and I didn't find it easy. I got up fairly regularly – not every day – but when I did get up, I didn't actually know what I was praying for; it was either in the Spirit or sometimes it seemed to be in silence. Sometimes there were actions, which I thought were a bit silly but that's what God seemed to require of me. I remember one day thinking that it might be more effective and helpful if I actually knew what I was praying, rather than praying in tongues. I said, "Lord, wouldn't it be better for me to know more about this, to know what I'm actually praying for, rather than so much of it being in tongues – wouldn't that be better?" The answer was immediate: "I need people who are just prepared to pray – I'll do the rest."

One thing I had to do was to pray that God would change my heart because I am by nature a very apathetic person. I had often thought, "Well, God's got it all in control anyway. What's the point in going on and on about it to him? He knows it. He's got the answers. He must get pretty bored with us asking." So I had to pray that he would change my heart; that he would remove my apathy; that he would make me care.

Slowly he did this and I began to have a heart for the things that he put there, to see things that I hadn't seen before. I actually began to see things supernaturally in a way that I hadn't done before. I had pictures and sometimes prophetic words which I'd not had before. In my personal life, in ministry, in praying for people, I felt a new kind of authority. The power of God was more evident. It was nothing that I did. It all came out of the intercession.

If you're someone who thinks you could never do it, that you'd never keep it up; if the enemy says to you, "Don't bother. You'd give up before you'd start" – be encouraged. It is now five years since I became 'seriously' involved in personal and corporate intercessory prayer. I fail often – not getting up, not doing it at home, not getting to the prayer meeting, but God's not there with a great big stick. You get out of it far more than you give. I think my Christian life has gained so much more from intercession. I would really say, "Go for it."

"At least when we hit rock bottom, can't we thank him that we've got a rock to hit?"

James Odgers *on praying in bad times*

How should we pray when we hit rock bottom? Let's not fool about with prayers that we think are somehow 'all right'. Let's cry out and pray what we feel. Then, let's keep on praying in the way that we prayed before we felt forsaken. Let's remember to do that, however hollow it may feel. Let's continue in obedience to pray and praise and worship. It isn't a question of feeling at this stage – this is a question of obedience.

We need to know that when God is silent, he is silent for a purpose. We need to know that when we hit rock bottom, although God's view of rock bottom for us may be rockier and more bottomy than where we think it is, there is something to hold on to. At least when we hit rock bottom, can't we thank him that we've got a rock to hit?

In 2 Samuel 22:2, it says, "The Lord is my Rock, my fortress and my deliverer. My God is my Rock in whom I take refuge, he is my stronghold, my refuge and my saviour." And Psalm 26:5 says, "Trust in the Lord forever for the Lord is the Rock eternal." That's what we hit when we hit rock bottom.

If you pray in tongues, then I recommend that you pray in tongues all the time or for as much of the time as you can. Why? Because I have found at least, that it is a reminder that God has good gifts for his children. Also, let's prepare now for these times to come. Now that we know they are going to come

because they do, they're part of God's plan which is perfect –
let's prepare now.

How? Firstly, by saturating ourselves in the Word of God –
Psalm 1 covers that. We are to meditate on the Bible day and
night, immersing ourselves in the Word of God. Then,
remember as many of the promises as we can for the dark,
silent times. Here are some: "I came that you might have life,
life in all its abundance." "Come unto me all you who are
weary and heavy laden, and I will give you rest." "It is for
freedom that Christ has set us free."

I find it useful as well, to keep a list of my answered prayers
and every other answered prayer I can get a hold of, so that I
can build a great wall like a wave, to flood into those desert
times when they come. The other thing is to ensure that we are
in a committed prayer relationship with at least one other
person so that we can share those times. They are likely to be
doing fine when we're hitting rock bottom. That's what
Christian fellowship is about, isn't it? It is to share the tough
times as well as the good times.

And as the saying goes, "Let us remember in the dark what
we learned in the light."

"It's ... the place of deepest intimacy where we can know and be known to the fullest."

Richard Foster *on prayer as an act of grace*

In the summer of 1990 I was working furiously on a book on prayer[1]. Of course there wasn't a book then – just a thousand jumbled ideas in my head and scrawled notes on scraps of paper. The university where I was teaching gave me a room in their library for that summer. They gave me a key so I could come and go any time of the day or night.

Over those months, I suppose I worked my way through 300 or so books in the field of prayer – classical books and contemporary books. Books, books, books. My head was just swimming with all of the debates about prayer, all of the divisions of prayer, all of the discussions and definitions of prayer. I had read everything I could lay my hands on about formation prayer, covenant prayer, adoration prayer, healing prayer, authoritative prayer, sacramental prayer. At one time, I had identified 41 major forms of prayer in the great devotional writers. I had studied every jot about Aratio, Lexio, Meditatio, Contemplatio, Silencio ...!

I'll never forget a night in July 1990. There I was in that library all alone. Everybody had left hours before. I had studied too much. It was too late. I'd worked too hard. I was experiencing overload. How could anybody deal with all of the intricacies and all of the difficulties of prayer in one book? There was just no way. I threw up my hands ready to abandon

---

[1] *Prayer: Finding the Heart's True Home*, Hodder and Stoughton

the project. "Forget it," I said. "The task is too daunting. The intricacies are too much. I just won't write the book."

Then something happened to me that is hard for me to express to you. The only way I know to say it is that I saw something, and what I saw was the heart of God, and the heart of God was an open wound of love. As best I can discern it, I heard the voice of the true Shepherd, not outwardly but inwardly, saying:

> I don't want you to abandon the project. Instead, I want you to tell my children that my heart is broken. Tell them I hurt at their distance and their pre-occupation. Tell them I mourn that they do not draw near to me. Tell them I grieve that they have forgotten me. Tell them I weep over their obsession with muchness and manyness. Tell them that I long for their presence.

So I'm telling you as best I can. I'm telling you how very much God desires our company. God is inviting you – God is inviting me – to come home to where we belong, to that for which we were created. His arms are stretched out wide to receive us. His heart is enlarged to take us in. You see, for too long we've been in a far country. It's been a country of 'climb and push and shove', a country of noise and hurrying crowds. He's inviting us to come home to peace, serenity, wholeness, intimacy, affirmation and care. We don't have to be afraid.

He welcomes us into the living room of his heart where we can put on old slippers and share freely. God invites us into the kitchen of his friendship where there is chatter and batter, mix and good fun. God welcomes us into the dining room of his strength where we can feast to our heart's delight. God welcomes us into the study of his wisdom where we can grow and stretch and ask all of the questions that we want. God welcomes us into the workshop of his creativity where we can become 'co-labourers with God', as Paul put it, working together to determine the outcome of events. God welcomes us into the bedroom of his rest where we can be open and vulnerable and free. It's also the place of deepest intimacy where we can know and be known to the fullest.

It doesn't matter if we have little faith or none. It doesn't matter if we're bruised and broken by the pressures of life. It doesn't matter if prayer has become cold and brittle to us. It doesn't matter. You see, God's arms are stretched out wide. We're welcome. We're welcome to come home because God accepts us – fully, freely, totally. Prayer is an act of grace because in it we discover that wonderful, loving, caring acceptance of God.

"Sing it to me again Daddy. Sing it to me again."

Richard Foster *gives an illustration of experiencing God's love*

Let me tell you about a friend of mine – Lymen James. He's a radio disc jockey and has a three-year-old son called Zachary. One day he and Zachary were out for an afternoon doing a little shopping. It was one of those days when nothing went right. Zachary was fussing and fuming and Lymen was trying everything. He tried to discipline him, he tried to be nice to him, he tried to get him candy and the candy was sticky. I mean, just nothing worked.

Finally – maybe under some special inspiration – Lymen scooped up Zachary and held him close to his chest and he started to sing a love song to him. He just made it up. The words didn't rhyme and he sang off-key but he just tried to share his love for his son with him. "I love you Zachary," he'd sing. "I'm glad you're my boy. I like to play ball with you. It's fun to see you smile." Things like that.

Zachary began to calm down and put his head on his father's shoulder. They kept going from place to place and Lymen quietly kept singing with words that didn't rhyme and were sung off-key. Zachary kept listening to this strange and exotic song. Finally, when they had finished for the afternoon and Lymen went back to the car to put his son into the seat, Zachary lifted up his head and he said, "Sing it to me again, Daddy. Sing it to me again."

Now you see prayer is a little like that. With simplicity of heart, we allow the great God of the universe to scoop us up and draw us close. We come to experience the heart of God – his love, his acceptance, his availability.

"Honey, I feel good. I haven't said that for 26 years have I?"

Richard Foster *on confession*

Many years ago, a middle-aged man came up to me with tears in his eyes. He said, "I'd like to speak with you." I said, "Sure." I set a time to go see him on a Thursday night. This man began to share his need and his brokenness.

He described how he had been in a deep sadness and sorrow for 26 years. He would wake up in the middle of the night in a cold sweat, screaming. He described how, during the Second World War, he'd been a ranger in Italy in charge of 33 men on a mission. They got pinned down by the enemy. He had prayed desperately all day long that God would get them out of there, but it wasn't to be. He had to send his men out, two by two, and watch them get killed. Finally, in the early hours of the morning, he was able to escape with six men. Four of them were seriously wounded. All he had was a little flesh wound. He told me he had become an atheist out of that experience. He was mad at God, full of guilt and anger.

I listened to that little story and my heart just went out to him. I said, "Don't you know that Jesus Christ, the Son of God who died for you, can set you free from that deep sadness, that sorrow, that brokenness." He didn't know! For twenty-six years, he didn't know. I came and sat on the couch beside him and put my hand on his shoulder (that was my shy way of laying on of hands) and I prayed a child-like little prayer. I didn't know how else to do it.

I just asked Jesus to walk back those 26 years with that man, to walk through that day and let him know that he loved him, that he was there, that he cared for him and to draw out the guilt, the hurt and the anger, and to set him free. And I added – I just thought of it, I guess – "Lord, I would be so appreciative if one of the evidences of this healing work would be for him to be able to sleep all night long." After about a half an hour, he turned to his wife and said, "Do you know, Honey, I feel good. I haven't said that for 26 years, have I?" She said, "No, you haven't."

The next Sunday, there he was. It was the second time in 26 years that he'd been in a church building. He came down the aisle three feet off the ground. He got a hold of me, lifted me up and said, "I slept all night long for three nights straight and every morning, I woke up with a hymn on my mind." That's the way confession can work. God's grace, God's mercy. That's the discipline of confession.

"There is nothing new about prayer for revival."

Jeremy Jennings *on the importance of praying for revival*

There is nothing new about prayer for revival. Unfortunately, from time to time in the life of every people and nation we get to that situation where revival is the only way forward, the only way out.

It seems like God, in his infinite wisdom, knew that from the very beginning or at least from early days. This passage in 2 Chronicles 7 says it all:

> When I shut up the heavens so that there is no rain, or command locusts to devour the land or send a plague among my people, if my people, who are called by my name, will humble themselves and pray and seek my face and turn from their wicked ways, then will I hear from heaven and will forgive their sin and will heal their land. (vv 13-14)

What God requires of his people is addressed to us. Corporate intercessory prayer preceded the Day of Pentecost. We are told in Acts 1 that the risen Jesus gave his disciples this command, "Do not leave Jerusalem, but wait for the gift my father promised, which you have heard me speak about. For John baptised with water, but in a few days you will be baptised with the Holy Spirit." If that had been me, I think I would have said, "Well, that's nice. So let's go and wait for this wonderful thing that is coming to pass."

But, for the people of God of that day that was not their reaction. Yes, they went to Jerusalem. Yes, they waited but they

did a third thing: "They all joined together constantly in prayer."
I don't think it is reading too much into the text here to presume
that having been promised the power of the Holy Spirit by
Jesus Christ, the thing they all joined together constantly in
prayer for was the coming of the Holy Spirit.

Poor conditions are ideal revival conditions. Revivals come
to the people of God when they are down and out – not when
they are in victory and churches are multiplying all over the
place. Isaiah 64 sums up this sense of desperation that we begin
to feel: "Oh, that you would rend the heavens and come down,
that the mountains would tremble before you!" (v 1) Then, like
the prophets, we find ourselves praying for the spirit of God to
pray through us. Prayers like this: "Oh, that you would rend the
heavens and come down." That is a statement of: we are desperate, we have tried just about everything we know. We have
formed committees in the church, we have written papers in the
church. We have tried human endeavour and human activity
and human wisdom in the church and none of it seems to be a
solution for the besetting problems that we are facing as a
people, as a church, as a nation.

So, we come to the point where we are desperate. I think that
is the point at which revivals are born – where we come to the
end of our tether and we reach the beginning of the power of
God. I would like to go on to consider some of the charac-
teristics of effective corporate intercession.

The first characteristic is **passion**. Speaking through the
prophet Joel, the Lord says, "Even now… return to me with all
your heart, with fasting and weeping and mourning. Rend your
hearts and not your garments." (Joel 2:12) It isn't about
models. It isn't about formulas. It is about the cry in the hearts
of the people of God, inspired and put there by the Spirit
of God.

The second characteristic is **unity**. We are seeking to
promote and develop unity. In that verse in Acts, they all joined
together constantly in prayer. They united in prayer. They were

all crying out to God to send his Holy Spirit. As the people of God seek to unite, looking up at him who is at our head, it seems to draw us closer together on the earth. It brings about a unity. That has been our experience in this activity.

We have had a number of occasions when a number of us have gone away for what we call 'Prayer Weekends'. One of the things that people have said most often after coming back from those weekends is that there was extraordinary unity amongst us as we sought what was on the heart of God together.

The third characteristic is **persistence**. Again in the Acts verse, there is that word 'constantly'. They didn't just pray once or twice. They were at this activity constantly until what they were waiting for had come to pass on the earth. In Luke 18:1 Jesus told his disciples a parable to show them that, "they should always pray and not give up". That speaks of persistence. This is something we are seeking to develop. We wouldn't claim to have arrived, nothing like it!

The fourth and final characteristic is **belief**. Jesus said, "Therefore I tell you, whatever you ask for in prayer, believe that you have received it, and it will be yours." (Mark 11:24) I also come back again and again to what the writer to the Hebrews says: "And without faith it is impossible to please God, because anyone who comes to him must believe that he exists and that he rewards those who earnestly seek him." (Hebrews 11:6)

We have discovered and learned three particular lessons in our limited experience in seeking to establish effective corporate intercessory prayer. The first thing we discovered was the **weekly meeting**. We began from very small beginnings. This current season of prayer in the life of this church [Holy Trinity Brompton] couldn't have begun from smaller beginnings. But we developed here, the 'one hour per week prayer meeting'. We need a regular meeting that calls for commitment. It calls for perseverance, for turning up. If it is at

7 am in the morning, it means getting up quite early. We now have a prayer meeting every weekday morning of the week but it has been a process.

Then we discovered the central role of **worship** in this activity. We see intercession and worship as being instrumental in piercing spiritual darkness. Then we have learnt in the context of corporate prayer meetings, the importance of **leadership**. Corporate prayer meetings need leading. They are all about the people of God uniting and pulling together. It is not about assembling a group of people and saying, "Just pray for anything you like now." There is no point in coming together to do that. We have, therefore, discovered the importance of these meetings being clearly led from the front.

We believe God is calling us to cry out to him for this land. Not just for those in the churches but for those outside the churches, who are on the wide road that leads to destruction. We are to pray for them. We are to pray for change in this land for their sake and for his sake, the author and the perfecter of our faith.

"It is not quite enough to know that we are to pray. What are we to pray?"

Sandy Millar *on finding God's purpose*

In the Apology of Aristides (c. 130 AD) we find the following reference to the prayer life of Christians of that time:

Now the Christians, Oh King, as men who know God, ask from him petitions which are proper for him to give and for them to receive; and thus they accomplish the course of their lives. And because they acknowledge the goodnesses of God towards them lo! on account of them there flows forth the beauty that is in the world.

Let us consider two of the thoughts in that paragraph: "….as men who know God…" and "petitions which are proper for him to give…"

It is very encouraging indeed to see the increased emphasis and excitement that there is today on prayer and intercession. Andrew Murray once wrote that, "the man who mobilises the Christian church to pray will make the greatest contribution in history to world evangelism".

This is even better. This is the Spirit of God himself mobilising the Christian church to pray – in large groups, small groups, in church, at work, as individuals, on our own. The church is stirred from within to want to pray – to be involved with God in bringing into existence plans that are clearly in the mind of God and which he is gradually unfolding as being things that he wants and intends to do in our time just as he did with the early church at the time at which Aristides was writing.

True prayer springs not from duty, guilt, remorse or fear but from love. From within that loving relationship of intimacy, many different people from many different backgrounds and churches today are sensing that **now** is the time to pray. **Now** is the time for concentrated prayer. But it is not quite enough to know that we are to pray. What are we to pray? Here are four things that I believe God is re-emphasising today. They are all "… petitions which are proper for him to give …"

Firstly, **it is God's will that everyone should know Jesus Christ.** In a light-hearted article in *The Times* recently, Matthew Parris wrote that, "Woolly-minded outlooks are to MPs what wet noses are to dogs – a sign of health." He could equally have been writing about some of us in the church. The gospel is universal and God is not slow in keeping his promise. But he is patient, "not wanting anyone to perish, but everyone to come to repentance." (2 Peter 3:9)

Put another way (this time by St Paul): He "wants all men to be saved and to come to a knowledge of the truth. For there is one God and one mediator between God and men; the man Christ Jesus."(1 Timothy 2:4-5). More significant even than this are the words of Jesus himself: "But I, when I am lifted up from the earth, will draw all men to myself." (John 12:32)

So don't let's waste a moment wondering if God really wants to see our particularly difficult neighbour saved, or his child, or a colleague at work or a cabinet minister or a school teacher etc. – he does! Let's pray imaginatively for every aspect of evangelistic opportunity that comes to our minds; for family, friends, for those involved in Alpha, missionaries, church workers, Earl's Court ministries, schools. The list is endless. Let's pray that the Lord of the harvest will send workers into his harvest field (Matthew 9:38) and bear in mind the very real possibility that we ourselves might turn out to be an answer to our prayers – without even having to move house.

Secondly, **it is God's will that all believers should grow spiritually.** Paul writes to the Christians at Colossae: "We have not stopped praying for you and asking God to fill you with the knowledge of his will through all spiritual wisdom and understanding." (Colossians 1:9) Perhaps you could have a group of friends praying specifically for Christian children, young people, schools, leaders, families, marriages, engagements. You could be praying into existence wise friends for them, people to encourage them – that they may grow into giants for God, pleasing him in every way, bearing fruit in every good work, growing in the knowledge of him, being strengthened with all power according to his glorious might.

St Augustine had the godly Monica (his mother) praying for him throughout his unregenerate youth. No doubt she met with other wives and Christian people, with what wonderful effect. I cannot see how young people, new Christians (or indeed any of us for that matter) can survive if we don't have selfless people pouring themselves out in prayer for us.

Thirdly, **it is God's will that all believers should become involved.** The purpose of God is that all God's people should be prepared for works of service. That is why God provided particular giftings to the church: apostles, prophets, evangelists, pastors and teachers. (Ephesians 4:11) There is thankfully no unemployment in the kingdom of God. There is no sitting around tasting sermons, expressing views like a sort of voyeuristic art critic who looks at things from a safe distance but never gets involved. There is an old poem that you may have heard which goes like this:

> Christ has no hands but our hands
> To do his work today.
> Christ has no feet but our feet
> To lead men in his way.
> Christ has no lips but our lips
> To tell men how he died.
> Christ has no love but our love
> To lead men to his side.
> We are the only Gospel
> The careless world will read.
> We are the sinner's Bible
> We are the scoffer's Creed.
> We are the Lord's last message
> Written in deed and word.
>
> What if the type be crooked?
> What if the print be blurred?
> What if our hands are busy
> With other work than his?
> What if our feet be going
> Where sin's allurement is?
> What if our lips be speaking
> Of things his lips would spurn?

How can we hope to win men
And hasten his return?

Will you start or join in with urgent prayer that every member of Christ's body, the church, today sees this? The only way to testify to the love of God that is in you is to pour it out and spend it on other people.

On the famous occasion just before the Ascension, when Jesus drew from Peter his thrice-repeated expression of love and thereby gave Peter confidence (among other things) to believe it himself, Jesus at the same time showed him how it could be made known in down-to-earth practical terms: "Feed my sheep!" That is, "Don't just talk about it. Do it!" Bedraggled, awkward, angular, difficult some of them may be, but sheep! For Jesus's sake and with his love, we are to love them as the expression of God's nature in us.

Fourthly, **it is God's will for all believers to live in, but not of, the world, in purity and growing holiness.** The writer to the Hebrews puts it more strongly I suspect, than most of us have taken in. "Make every effort to live in peace with all men and to be holy; without holiness no-one will see the Lord." (Hebrews 12:14) Oh, that we might have 150 groups of people – large or small – by the end of this year meeting together to pray for some of these things.

May I appeal to you to pray into existence the extraordinarily wonderful purposes of God for his church today? What could be more exciting than that?

Faith's challenges

"God gave me a song: 'Not the strongest will win, but those who trust in Christ.'"

Paul Negrut *on his life as a Christian in Romania*

I was the third boy in my family. My parents were farmers when the Communists came and took everything – the land, the cattle, the tools and forced my mother and father to work the land for them. A farmer would get a kilo of grain as a wage for a hard working day on a farm.

In that situation, farmers were not looking for more babies. My parents didn't want another one because they already had two and they couldn't feed them – and then I came. This was a big problem for the family because my mum, after she gave birth, was not allowed to stay home and nurse me. She was forced on the field to work the land for the Communists. Otherwise they would not even get that kilo of wheat and they would be prosecuted for sabotage. So when I was two weeks old, my mum had to wake up and go on the field and work. I was left alone all day because there was no-one to look after me.

When I was two months old, I got ill and was in a coma for two weeks. My parents were forced to work every day on the field. They were not allowed to take me to a doctor. The nearest medical office was about 15 miles away, over hills and valleys in another larger village, and my parents were not allowed to take me to that doctor because it would take a whole day.

So after two weeks when my father saw that I did not die, he couldn't bear any more of that situation. He said to my mum, "Even if they kill me, I'm taking this boy to a doctor to see what is the matter with him," but he had no transportation. So with the help of some neighbours, they put together a sort of cart which was almost falling apart. They put some hay on it and put me on it, and my father set off for that village. Half way there, I opened my eyes, maybe because of the bumpy road and my dad was so happy that he turned back home, so I never saw a doctor. But today, I know that this life that I have now is not mine.

The first time I saw butter in my life was when I was 16. I had my first overcoat when I was 16. I saw the wickedness, the injustice, the evils and I grew up with rebellion in my heart. I was determined to go my own way. That created a big problem especially if I tell you that I was good at doing things my own way. I was successful in school at everything I did. When you are rebellious and successful, that moves you away from God and the only thing that I was not willing to acknowledge was that I had to kneel down before God and let him rule my life.

When I was 15, my parents moved from that village to the city of Oradia, where my father got a very poor job. Soon, I identified a group of other rebellious teenagers and I mixed with them and we lived in rebellion. When I was 16, I met a young girl – she was 15. That young girl is now my wife. I do not encourage young people to date that early in life so please do not take my example as an excuse.

She came from a different background. She lost her father when she was nine, and her mum remained without job, social security, or any financial or material support. But she was a godly woman and she lived by prayer. She prayed every day that God would feed her and her nine-year-old daughter. They lived by prayer, and every day God answered their prayers and cared for them.

When my girlfriend saw my rebellious way, she tried to

minister to me but I was determined to resist. She was very kind and waited patiently for the time to come but I was not willing to take the religious way. When I graduated from High School, I decided to go into the military and be an officer – an army secret police officer. Then my girlfriend spoke to me and said, "Paul, I spent a few weeks away in the summer and I met a clinical psychologist." In that moment, there was a light inside my heart. I looked at her and said, "I will study clinical psychology."

So I applied for the University of Bucharest, the only one that had a department of clinical psychology. In order to be registered at a university in Romania for clinical psychology, you need a paper from the Communist party headquarters saying that you are not a Christian. So I went to the Communist party and asked for that paper and since the organisation knew me as a rebel, they were not worried about giving it to me. In 1972 when this happened, there were only 90 places in the clinical psychology department, and there were 2,500 applicants.

I had to pass the entry examination and in Romania, entrance examinations are very difficult. They have two parts – written and oral. For the written test, we were divided into rooms and the professor came and wrote on the blackboard the topics of the essays that we were supposed to write. So I did my best – I wrote whatever I remembered but it was very little and I got a very bad mark. In Romania, marks are from 0-10. 0 is the lowest, 10 is the highest. When the essays were marked, I got 6 which was very low because ahead of me were at least 500 between 7 and 10, and there were only 90 places.

That was the first time in my life that I was confronted with myself and I had failed. I was so discouraged, depressed and ashamed I couldn't face that, so I decided to commit suicide. It seemed the only way to get out of the mess. I packed everything in a small case and wrote a note for my parents telling them what had happened. But before I left the room where I was staying during the exam, I remembered what my girlfriend had told me when I went. She said, "Paul, whenever you come to the end of yourself, remember that then the grace of God will begin for you." I realised that I was at the end of myself and I fell to the ground, agonising and crying out to God. I was not trained in religious matters, but I was there for hours.

When I woke up I was a changed man. There was a deep peace in my heart. My mind was clear and, more than that, God gave me a song with words and music which remained in my mind for two weeks. The words were: "Not the strongest will win, but those who trust in Christ."

With that assurance, I went to the oral examination, although humanly speaking there was no hope. In those days, the oral examination was very crazy in Romania. There was a huge wooden table like in the Kremlin, with five professors behind the table and the table was filled with small pieces of paper like in a lottery. The students picked two pieces of paper, looked at the topics and, out of their heads, had to say whatever they knew about those topics. The professors would stop you, turn you upside down and confuse you because they had to dismiss 2,410 and select only 90.

So I picked two pieces of paper and I looked at my topics, and I thought that the whole world was caving in on me because I had no idea what it was all about. I thought I'd better throw away the papers and run away. In that struggle, there was a voice inside me which said, "Why don't you take a seat?" I turned round and there was a seat there and a small desk; I took that seat and I began to cry out to God again to help me. Then there was an audible voice and that voice dictated my topics. I took up my pen and began to write, very quickly to keep in step with the voice. When the voice stopped, the examiner said, "Negrut, it's your turn, come here and answer."

I began to read my paper because that was all I could do. I read very quickly to give them no time to stop me but as I was reading, they were speechless! I remember looking quickly to see what was happening with those draculas behind the desk; I thought that what I was saying was so stupid, they'd lost their voices. I kept reading.

When I finished reading the first topic, they asked me who my father and mother were, and who trained me for that exam, what kind of books I had and where I got those ideas from. My answer was that I had no professors, no brothers in the Communist party – nothing! Then one examiner asked me what my mark had been in the written test and I told him it was 6. He seemed concerned. Then he said, "Do you know something about your second topic?" I took my notes and I read the second topic. When I'd finished he stood up, shook my hand over that huge desk and said, "Mr Negrut, I am so pleased that you are my student." He gave me the mark 10! It was the only mark 10 that was given in 1972 in the University of Bucharest, Department of Clinical Psychology, at the oral examination. My wife asked me to be sure that whenever I speak about that 10, to remember that it is Jesus's. 10. It's God who gets that 10!

So there I was with a paper that said I wasn't a Christian – and now I was a Christian. Although I had failed my exam I was admitted as a student. I went back home and my girlfriend met me at the railway station and asked me what had happened. I told her and she said, "Paul, we have to tell all our friends what happened." Seventeen of them accepted Jesus when I told them what had happened and were all baptised together in the time of the Communist persecution.

Within a few weeks I started my first academic year. The first course we had was an introduction to atheism. There was a chap telling us that Jesus never existed, that God doesn't exist and that it was myth and not reality. I was boiling inside – how could somebody say that? After a few lectures, I stopped him and said, "Can I suggest to you some books to read about the historical records of Jesus of Nazareth?" He stopped me and called me to the Communist Party office and said, "Shut up! If you open your mouth once again, you are out of this school."

Next time he came to our class, he looked over the classroom and said, "I want to ask you a question. Who believes in God? Please raise your hand." I knew he was after me. If I raised my hand, I would be expelled from school because you are not allowed to study if you are a Christian. By that time I was so confused – I knew that God existed but I was not willing to lose my opportunity to study. I think that in those moments, I understood the apostle Peter when he looked at that servant lady and denied Christ. I was almost ready to deny Christ.

As I was crying out for help not to compromise, I was willing myself to raise my hand. I raised my eyes first to look around and all my colleagues were there with their hands up! They told me later that they knew I was a Christian and that the professor was there to spot me and expel me. They said, "Paul, we felt that we should protect you" and I was the last one to put my hand up! By that time, the professor was so shocked that he looked at one of the best students in our class and said, "Demetrius, are you a Christian?" and Demetrius said, "Mr Professor, Hegel believed in God, Kant believed in God, Heideger believed in God. Mr Professor, who are you that you claim that you do not believe in God compared to those great philosophers?" The professor left!

I graduated from the University of Bucharest as an expert in clinical psychology, and when I was in my last year I married that girl. She is my wife and we have two beautiful daughters.

"I didn't want to become a pastor because I knew what it meant to be a pastor in a Communist country."

Paul Negrut *on life under persecution*

As soon as I started my job as a clinical psychologist, the secret police were after me. They sent a secret police officer into my office every day. He was in my office eight hours a day watching over me. Whatever I said, whatever I did, he was hunting for something, so he could claim that I used my office for religious purposes. How can you live a Christian life when he is there to identify that you live a Christian life? It is not easy. I will not go into details, but after almost eight years in that office with persecutions and all sorts of threats, God called me into full-time pastoral ministry.

I didn't want to become a pastor because I knew what it meant in a Communist country. I had seen what happened to our pastors before and I was not willing. Again, in a miraculous way, God spoke to me and he forced me into the pastoral ministry. He helped me all the way through.

In 1988, due to the persecution and the pressures that were on us, I had a stroke. I was paralysed, I couldn't move my hand and my left foot, yet three months later I was on my feet again in the pulpit preaching the gospel. Some months later, my wife had a stroke and she too was restored. I then had a second stroke. By that time, the secret police decided to attack us through our children. I will not tell you what they did because I want to protect my family, but it is enough to tell you that one night when I came home, I saw that my family was crushed. My eldest daughter couldn't speak, she was so shocked. She was terrified.

When I saw what they did, I felt that God was unjust with me. I thought God was unfair. I said, "Lord, I know why I am suffering, my wife knows why she's suffering, but this girl doesn't know. She's not yet at an age to make a decision. You aren't fair!" I was angry with God and wanted to leave Romania. Many people crossed the borders of Romania illegally in those days escaping to the western world, so I worked out a plan that I would take my family out and I said, "Lord, I care for this family more than you do."

I went to speak to a friend of mine and told him what happened and what I was going to do. I shared with him all my failures and all my disappointments with God. He said, "Paul, wait here and I will come later to speak to you." He came with an old piece of paper in his hand and said, "Paul, read this letter." It was written by a man who spent 25 years in prison. Tortured every day and after 25 years, because the Communists couldn't break him down, they executed him. Before they murdered him – he knew that this would happen to him – he managed to write a last letter; it was given to his cellmate and somehow, through God's grace, it came out and reached that man's family.

The letter was actually a prayer. It said, "Dear Lord, I know that my time is coming to an end and very soon I am going to see you face to face." Then he developed his idea of the glory of heaven. He described it in his imagination saying, "Lord, I can hardly wait to see all your family together. I can hardly wait to see all your great evangelists and great servants, to see the missionaries, the choirs, singers and all those who serve you. Especially Lord, I can hardly wait to see that moment when the martyrs will come with their crowns and they will lay down their crowns at your feet. Lord, in that day grant me a special favour. Lord, let me come to that heavenly procession in the uniform of a Romanian prisoner because I want to praise you for all eternity as a prisoner for Christ."

That was his last prayer. When I read that letter, I was broken inside; I knelt down and I prayed saying, "Lord, give me that grace, that I praise you for all eternity as a Romanian for Christ. It would be so easy to praise you today as an American for Christ, as a German for Christ, as an Englishman for Christ but give me the grace to praise you as a Romanian for Christ."

I went home and spoke to my wife and we prayed together. We decided to praise God for all eternity as Romanians. We decided to stay in Romania. Despite more pressures and more persecution, God took care of us and he always gave us enough grace. Now, the gospel is proclaimed on television in Romania and we receive up to 30,000 letters every day from people who have heard the gospel through our ministry on television. When I see the gospel of Christ proclaimed in Romania, I praise him as the Lord of history.

~

"I was absolutely frightened out of my wits for all 43 treatments..."

John Wimber *on his experiences of radiation treatment for cancer of the throat*

On April 6, 1993 I was diagnosed as having a cancer of the nasal pharynx. Shortly after that, I began radiation treatment – 43 treatments over the next two months. Sometime in mid-July, I finished the treatment and I was told that if this particular type of cancer were going to re-occur, it would probably re-occur within the first two years.

Most people are given a five-year span but evidently this type comes back quicker if it's going to come back. On April 9, 1994 I was examined and told that I had no evidence of any cancer at all in my body. In July 1995, I was through the first year of waiting so now I'm into my second year. [He was speaking in the autumn of 1995.]

I have some limitations. I don't have saliva glands, so it's difficult for me to talk for protracted periods of time. Without saliva, you don't digest food very well, so I get raw food into my stomach and that means I have constant heartburn and stomach aches; I've lost over a hundred pounds – about eight stone – so that's a lot of weight. I'm very weak. When you starve, you don't lose fat, you lose muscle so I've very little muscle on my body. I fall over every now and then. I haven't done it much lately because I've been doing limited exercise in the last two months. I don't sleep well, I've lost a little bit of memory – sometimes radiation does that – and I've lost a major part of my hearing, about 80% in my left ear and about 60% in my right. But they say I may recoup my hearing – it has to do with fluid. In fact, in the last month I have had intermittently better hearing. Some days I can hear better than others. Right now, I feel I'm at the sea shore. I'm 61 and that's not so old but as I have said, it's not the model it's the mileage. I've been very compulsive in my life and I'm a workaholic. I've worked too hard for years.

A question that has often been asked me is, "Did you commune with the Lord through this time?" Commune with the Lord?! I was unconscious, I slept 20/22 hours a day. They had to carry me out of the bed to get the treatment. They put me under this thing and they clamped this other thing over my head. I found out that I was claustrophobic. They took straps and put them over me. You have to be totally immobilised for this treatment because radiation is an exact art and if they miss, they could fry your brain in a few seconds. I was absolutely frightened out of my wits for all 43 treatments, not just one time.

But the Lord was there in the midst of the fear, in the midst of the panic, in the midst of the horror. He was always there. He didn't remove the horror. He didn't remove the panic. I think he could have. He could have healed me of the claustrophobia but he didn't. I've heard of people who fall asleep under that machine. They enjoy the activity but for me they may as well have hung me from a 20-storey building by my heels as far as fright was concerned. But in the midst of that, God met me every time. Radiation is hell. It's the worst thing I've ever experienced in my life. It is utterly devastating. The cancer you're not really aware of. The radiation and the after-effects? You're aware of nothing else.

But God carried me through it and taught me some wonderful things. I realise that much of my life and much of the body of Christ has assumed the avoidance of pain is one of the blessings of being a Christian. I have found just the opposite – that the embracing of pain is one of the blessings of being a Christian. When I have gone through devastating tests and trials like that, all of them have produced great dividends in my life. Most of the growth that's ever occurred in my life has occurred in the midst of great pain: the loss of loved ones, the betrayal of people that have left me, the immorality in the lives of close confidants and colleagues, the devastation of sickness. I'm profoundly proud of God and his willingness to meet us at those deep and dark times of life.

But when I was going through the treatment, it wasn't a time of advancing faith. I couldn't even focus my eyes, so I couldn't read Scripture. Thank God, I had memorised lots of Scripture when I was younger and the few minutes I was awake, I would think about Scripture and I would always wake to the sense of God's presence in the room. There was always that sense of God's immediate presence and I grew a new awareness and appreciation of what it means to be in the presence of the Lord. He went with me through that. He did not abandon me but he also didn't save me from it. So it was obviously his choice, his sovereign will, that I go through that – and I accept his sovereign will.

"You'll have just enough of Jesus to be miserable unless you have all of him and he has all of you."

Ken Costa *on backsliding*

Why did Peter backslide so badly? This is an important question because you and I need to watch it. We need to be careful that we don't go exactly the same way. Peter was so close to Jesus but he denied him. He was a traitor to him. He turned his back on him. Now how did that come about?

This is the history of the collapse: in Matthew 26:31, Jesus gets up at the Last Supper and tells Peter, "This very night you will fall away on account of me." Peter replies, "I never will." Jesus says (v 34), "This very night you will disown me three times." Peter declares (v 35), "I will never disown you." Now what happens when Jesus says one thing and we say another? The point is he disbelieved the word of the Lord. That is the first step. Now when the word of the Lord comes to you, whether in the Scriptures or through a friend or whatever, take care. That isn't the moment to say, "No, it's not." Because this is where Peter's first mistake was: **he disbelieved the word.**

Second, Matthew 26:43 tells us Peter was drowsy in prayer. It's a tragedy. Jesus is sweating blood in Gethsemane and he asks them to pray – and three times they are asleep. The closest friends he has desert him. They are sleeping at Jesus's moment of agony. You ought to ask yourself this question: how do you walk with someone for three years and have him sweat blood and not realise that 'this is the moment that I must be with you'. And Peter was not. He was drowsy in prayer. Jesus wanted them to watch and pray. That's the second step: **they stopped**

praying. Sleep and other things took over, and the backsliding is now beginning to get really quite serious. What is happening is that Jesus is preparing himself at the critical moment of his life for a very important event and when he says in verse 46, "Rise, let us go" he means, "We are now ready and prepared – or at least I am." But Peter was not.

Look at what happens next. He had disbelieved the word; he was drowsy in prayer and now he was distracted by the flesh. Because as soon as Jesus is set upon, Peter (John's gospel tells us) takes the sword out of his scabbard and cuts off the ear of the High Priest's servant. It was a 'magnificent gesture' and 'great attack upon the centres of power'. He takes the sword and what does he do? He *cuts off the ear...* a massively irrelevant act! Because Peter by then is driving on human overdrive. What else can you do when you are not listening to the Lord, when you are not praying? **You are going to be distracted by the flesh** which is strong within us. Here is the old, tempestuous, strong Peter who rushes out and believes that in his own strength he can take the sword and make an act on behalf of Jesus; do something to protect Jesus. It is a complete irrelevance. That's what we do quite often in our own lives. We go into our own strength. We start striving away thinking, "God, I'm really doing you a favour." We don't pray, we don't listen, we don't talk to him and we think we're OK. No doubt Peter thought he was OK too.

Then what happens? He is distracted by the flesh and then in verse 58 it says, "Then Peter followed him... at a distance." **He distances himself from his friend.** He's in trouble. Oh my, he's in trouble.

That is where backsliding starts in our own lives. We start drawing away from Jesus. That intimacy isn't there any more. You are not necessarily going to say he's the greatest man in the world. There is no way in which you or I is going to survive in a world as hostile as the one we have to live in at a distance, I promise you. Don't even try it. You'll just have enough of

Jesus to be miserable. If you can only catch him in passing, don't catch him at all. If you can only just see him come up to you, don't bother. Because the only place to have him is right in your heart and next to you. You'll have just enough of Jesus to be miserable unless you have all of him and he has all of you.

Peter not only distances himself from Jesus, he deserts him. Verse 58 tells us he follows him at a distance, he enters the courtyard and he sits down with the guards to see the outcome. Peter has become a spectator. Do you see that? He comes to watch the outcome. This just cracks me up. It is the same thing that I do: "Please God, move by your Spirit in this place and I'll just watch the outcome. I don't really want to get involved. The homeless are pretty nasty and smelly. I don't really want to be where you are Lord. I want to be in the nicer places." Then verse 69, you know the terrible story. He sits in the courtyard; they are cold and try to warm themselves, but by then there is no amount of human or circumstantial warmth that can warm Peter's heart. His heart has gone cold. His light has gone out. The cock crows and Peter curses by his own name that he has never met or seen this man, and not to the High Priest, but to some servant girl in the outer court of the High Priest's chamber.

I think Peter is so much like us. We just sit out there denying Jesus every day – in our work, our discussions, our talks, our holding back, our commitment, in our lives. Then Peter goes out and weeps; he dissolves as a person. This is the absolute crash – you don't go lower than this – he 'wept bitterly'. Then, you see, he was a broken man. Peter, the strong tempestuous man, was shown to be completely irrelevant to the historical drama that was unfolding. His contribution to this great moment in the life of the Master was to cut the ear off the slave of the High Priest. That was the first leader of the Christian Church.

This comes to all of us in our Christian lives. For some of you it is happening now. You are registering and ticking these things off. But even when Peter went to that lowest point, he wasn't without his God and friend. Because even though he had abandoned his Lord and Master, Jesus Christ had not abandoned him. He'd been called, he'd been commissioned, he collapsed and he received the charge from Jesus at the end of John.

In John 21, here is Jesus at his most gracious reinstating Peter. What does Peter feel? He's sold out. He sits there with Jesus having breakfast and when they have finished eating, Jesus says to Peter, "Simon, son of John, do you truly love me more than these?" And here is the reverse thrust – three times he asks that question, as if by each absolution to wipe the crow of the cock. For every denial, there was an affirmation.

"Feed my lambs"; "Take care of my sheep", says Jesus to him and six weeks later a man gets up on the day of Pentecost convinced by the Spirit. In Acts 2:14 it says, "Then Peter stood up with the Eleven, raised his voice and addressed the crowd..." Where does this new confidence come from? It comes from the work of God the Holy Spirit; it comes from the graciousness of God the Father, who takes hold of Peter and says, "I will reconstruct your life."

Peter in his own strength would have been a disaster to the church. Can you imagine what would have happened? Jesus is gone and it's, "Swords out chaps. Here we go, let's murder a High Priest." Peter had to see the death of Peter the Strong Man in order for a new vision to arise. That is when God says, "This is the vision I give to you" and that vision will be based squarely on the power of the Holy Spirit. Because as he disassembles us, so by his Spirit he reassembles us piece by piece in order that we might be the broken, suffering, but powerful witnesses to Jesus in this world. That's what happened to Peter. You'll have just enough of Jesus to be miserable unless you have all of him and he has all of you.

The first words spoken to Peter and the last words spoken to Peter by Jesus, were the same. In Mark 1:17, Jesus says,

"Come, follow me," and in John 21:19, he said to him, "Follow me." Then the very last words in verse 22, "You must follow me." The start of the life of Jesus and the end of his life – the same words, "Follow me" and never does that change for the life of you and me. Never – from the beginning of our lives as a Christian, to the middle point and to the end point; it will always be the same – follow the person of Jesus.

"Stress substitutes other relationships for the one which is dependent on the living God."

Ken Costa *on combating stress*

The actor John Cleese once wrote a book with his psychiatrist entitled, *Life and how to survive it.* Cleese started his psychoanalysis when he believed he was suffering from a pathological inability to enjoy life. But Dr Anthony Clare, host of the programme *In the Psychiatrist's Chair,* says of him, "He claims to have been freed of inhibition by psychotherapy, yet his three marriages remain largely murky and unexposed areas of private emotion, for all the transatlantic personal honesty."

If you leave this evening with one message, it should be this: that apart from Jesus Christ, I don't believe we have any hope of surviving the tensions that are breaking up our society at the moment. The self-help books may help you to adjust or to accommodate yourself to the prevailing pressures but they cannot help to transcend or to overcome them, which is the heritage of the sons and daughters of Jesus Christ alone.

Stress is universal. Just look at some of the **sociological**

stress around us – death, the loss of a loved one, moving house, family gatherings at Christmas. Then look at **sexual stress**. The pressure to have a relationship whether it works or not is endemic at the moment. Then there is the loneliness of a single person faced with pressure from peers. Thirdly, **secular stress** – am I in the right job? The amount of time that is spent working out whether you are in the right job, is an extraordinary fruitless activity for 80% of the enquiries that go on. We need to discover for ourselves the restfulness of believing that God has brought us into one position and that in due course, if we love and trust him, he will move us on. There is also financial strain. Whether it is that your house is valueless and the debt is high, or whether you're just tossing away the Barclaycard bills when they arrive because you don't dare face them. Fourthly, there is **spiritual stress** – striving in your own strength to accomplish God's purposes on earth. All with the best of intentions. People's hearts are wanting to go along but the striving to achieve it is ahead of God's plan.

What are the consequences of stress? The terrible thing about stress and pressure is that it takes our eyes off the right relationship with God. I've noticed an interesting phenomenon: when stress levels rise, there is a coarseness in personal relationships. Amazingly, selfishness in the most unselfish of people suddenly rises. Stress substitutes other relationships for the one which is dependent on the living God. That is its insidiousness. Stress in the spiritual sense, kills.

But the interesting thing is to look at Jesus because he is our model. There can be no other place to start. Jesus knew what it was like to be hemmed in, to have pressure tightening around him, and yet Jesus had a plan for survival. I am deeply struck by that extraordinary example in Luke 4:28-30, just after Jesus preaches the first sermon in Nazareth. Jesus turned on the people and said that they would not accept him. An extraordinary hue and cry breaks out and they drive Jesus out of the town, and take him to the top of a hill to throw him down from the cliff. The crowd has turned but Jesus (v 30) "walked right through the crowd and went on his way".

It is astonishing sovereignty, isn't it? Here is God in Christ, when all the pressure hems him in. He doesn't duck. He doesn't go for cover. He doesn't out-flank them. He just walks through the midst of that crowd. His sovereign authority is available to us in exactly the same way today. In Christ Jesus, when pressure hems us in we walk through the midst of it. Will it be troublesome? Sure. Will it be difficult? Of course. But will we overcome it? Yes! Why? Because Jesus did it and on the cross, won for us the right to walk in through him.

David the psalmist knew the same feeling. If you look at Psalm 18, you'll find this extraordinary sense that David knows. Verse 6 says, "In my distress I called on the Lord," and then verse 19, which has meant more to me in a hard working environment than almost any on the subject, "He brought me out into a spacious place, he rescued me because he delighted in me." Again in Psalm 31:8, "You have not handed me over to the enemy, but have set my feet in a spacious place." Don't you long for that when pressure is upon you? One of the things I have been studying carefully is that wonderful interchange that Mary had with the servants at the marriage feast in Cana. They came up and said, "There's no wine. What are we to do?" Mary then says these absolutely marvellous words, "Do whatever he tells you." If you had a stress strategy, that would be it.

We need emotionally enriching friendships. Elijah was sent Elisha to be his friend and Paul was sent Titus. David was given Jonathan and Jesus had John, the disciple whom he loved. An emotionally enriching friendship means precisely that. It isn't someone who's going to wag a spiritual finger at you all the time. It's someone you feel comfortable with, who builds you up. We all need it – and particularly in times of stress. We also need to determine those things which are not of God and cut them out of our lives, whether they are in relationships, a work place, or wherever. Cut it out! Recognise that Jesus knew the dependence on the Father and say, "That's what I'm going to do. Whatever I see the Father doing, I will do – no more and no less." Just do the anointed work.

Jesus said, "I know where I came from, and where I am going." (John 8:14) You must believe in your calling. Those who believe in themselves as Christ has modelled them, believe that there is a plan for good and not for evil in their lives. Those are the ones who are able to rest in the Lord, to wait patiently for him. Jesus only did anointed work. Is what you are doing anxious activity or anointed activity? If it's anxious activity, you are going to be stressed out. I am sorry but there are no solutions. We will love you through it but there's nothing we can offer until the relationship is set right. Anointed activity is that activity in which you do whatever he asks you to do. Sometimes you don't hear right. Sure, but at least the heart is right.

Jesus did what he saw the Father doing. No more. Our temptation is to do more than God is doing. It's a very stressful thing to fulfil the calling of someone else. It's an endemic problem to Christians who believe they are called to do what they're doing but really they want to be a worship leader and strum a guitar. "I'd long to do that," they say. If I'm called to children's work, then I want to be with grown ups. If I'm called into the City, then I want to be a clergyman. You can't fulfil the calling of another which is why it's so important to say, as Jesus did, "I can do nothing without the one who shows me. For the Father loves the Son and shows him all he does." That's the answer.

"Idols offer comfort."

David Parker *on how idols provide a false security*

Typically in the modern world, adults are looking for security and significance – the very things that God has called us to in Christ. You can see how so many people get stuck in what they look to for comfort. When we experience pain, fear, anxiety or pressure, opposition or hostility, sorrow, loss, rejection or alienation – or whatever – we need comfort. In the fall, we were born as insecure beings and unless we get healed and changed we will struggle with the issue of idolatry.

What's the connection here? It's this: idols offer comfort. Zechariah 10:2 says, "Idols speak deceit. Diviners see visions that lie. They tell dreams that are false. They give comfort in vain." What idols do is lie. They give apparent comfort but ultimately it's empty, unsatisfying and worthless. What idols provide is a false comfort, a clinging to worthless things that forfeits the grace that could otherwise be ours.

Now what kind of things could be false idols? The amazing thing about the subtlety of the modern world is that many of the things that become idols to us are not idols in themselves but are actually the means of comfort for our lives given by God. It's our looking to them as the principal source of comfort which makes them idols.

What are they? Firstly, **food**. Food is a genuine source of comfort from God but how many people turn to food as the main source of comfort in their life when they are in distress? It's a false comfort when it becomes the source. Secondly, **material security and financial power.** This is much more obvious to me in America than here; your typical middle-class

American person, when they get under stress or pressure goes shopping. "Let's go buy something to make us feel better. Let's go exercise some material acquisition and financial power and get some comfort into our lives." When money becomes the focus of our comfort we are dealing with a very significant idol indeed.

Thirdly, **sexual satisfaction**. This is one of the biggest idols of our time – the belief that if you are not sexually satisfied daily on numerous occasions, then you're going to turn blue and die; if you do not satisfy your sexual cravings you will be completely unhealthy. It is an absolute lie and it comforts in vain. Is sexual intimacy, in the context of marriage, not a given thing of God as a source of comfort? My experience tells me that yes, it is. But outside of that place, there is a serious problem of idolatry with sexual gratification. It has become a main source of comfort in people's lives and it's a completely false idol. There is a tremendous addiction in our culture to pornography and masturbation but I don't believe the seriousness of it lies in its perversion. The seriousness lies in its idolatry.

Fourthly, **entertainment** – fantasy, the movies, television, books, magazines, the escape from reality. The popularity of science fiction and fantasy is because it has become a source of comfort for people and it too comforts in vain. Fifthly, **alcohol and drugs**. Are not drugs a form of comfort given by God for when we are sick? Absolutely, but there is a whole generation that is looking to Ecstasy to provide what only the Holy Spirit can. It is looking to alcohol to give what only the relationship with the Father can provide. Lastly, **praise and approval of friends** and co-workers. Is that not a legitimate comfort? Why else would Hebrews tell us to encourage each other daily? But when we are addicted to the affirmation of others, it becomes an idolatrous relationship which offers nothing to us in the long run.

What's the true source of comfort then? What did Jesus say

in John 14? He said, "I will ask the Father and he will give you another Comforter to be with you for ever – the Spirit of truth which I have told you about." We have got to get in touch as Christian people with the genuine comforting role of the Holy Spirit in our lives. I think the major issue for most Christians is coming into that place of receiving comfort from the Lord. I don't mean to condemn in any way but today I believe, the Lord says, "You got idols? Burn them. Destroy them. Tell yourself they are not going to comfort you any longer." So many times in my ministry people, have said to me, "This thing, it controls me. What do I do? Do I need deliverance?" Sometimes that's true but most times it's not. The first step towards really getting comforted by God is to cut ourselves off from idols.

"...there was a beautiful four- or five-year-old girl ... and I knew she belonged to me."

David Parker *explains how God prepared him for his wife's miscarriage*

Before my wife got pregnant, I had a dream. In this dream I was standing at a fence and there was a beautiful four- or five-year-old girl and I knew she belonged to me. It wasn't one of my two daughters. I looked at her and she looked at me, and I wept because she wasn't with me and I didn't understand why. I knew that our family was going off in one direction and she was staying there.

After I woke up, I told my wife about the dream and I said, "I don't have a clue what this means but maybe the Lord wants to give us another child." We were really happy before that, I mean, four is plenty! But I thought, maybe the Lord is telling us there was one more that belongs with us that we should open our heart to. So we prayed and opened our hearts and lo, and behold, Nancy became pregnant.

Then, we come to this point – the sadness of losing this child, which I held in my hands; that three-inch-long infant with perfectly formed arms and legs and face. I knew that this was the little girl I saw. In the dream, I had that same feeling of, "I don't understand why you're not with me and why you're not going with us but I'll leave you to God." I tell you, the comfort of having the Spirit speak to me about this little child in advance, provided more foundation under me than all the meals and kindness that so many of you have shown me. Not that I don't need all that, but the reality is, this is a role of the Holy Spirit – to comfort our lives. He speaks to us and embraces us. We can feel him and know him, and he's with us always.

"Compassion cannot remain inactive."

Tom Gillum *on the response of a compassionate person to suffering*

Some time later the son of the woman who owned the house became ill. He grew worse and worse, and finally stopped breathing. She said to Elijah, 'What do you have against me, man of God? Did you come to remind me of my sin and kill my son?' 'Give me your son,' Elijah replied. He took him from her arms, carried him to the upper room where he was staying, and laid him on his bed. Then he cried out to the Lord, 'O Lord my God, have you brought tragedy also upon this widow I am staying with, by causing her son to die?' Then he stretched himself out on the boy three times and cried to the Lord, 'O Lord my God, let this boy's life return to him!' The Lord heard Elijah's cry, and the boy's life returned to him, and he lived. Elijah picked up the child and carried him down from the room into the house. He gave him to his mother and said, 'Look, your son is alive!' (1 Kings 17:17-23)

Elijah's compassion on the death of this young child comes out in two particular ways: first with action and secondly, with prayer. Compassion always leads to action. As your heart is pained with the fact it is a person that's suffering, there is a cry from within that says, "I've got to do something to help." There is an urge that simply won't allow you to stay sitting where you are. Also, there are no glib words. That is one thing a compassionate person will avoid.

On 7th April 1983, all five children of a Nigerian hospital chaplain who worked in Bradford died in a fire at his home. In one half hour spell, he lost all his children and his home. He spoke about the ghastliness of what he was going through saying, "It was a disaster. It was untidy. It was illogical, horrible and shocking – an affront to life. My world turned upside down. Reactions? Horror, shock, anger, utter disgust at life's cruelty. There was one lobby which saw the children's death as God's will, to which I could only respond with a certainty that it was not. Then there were those who felt that it was a judgement or some form of holy treat that we'd been selected for."

I know how easy it is to come up with a glib word, because you feel the need to say something and you feel the need to justify on God's behalf. You find yourself saying things which often come out in the most unhelpful and awkward ways. I've learnt the hard way by finding myself saying things and before you know it, they are deeply unhelpful. When I'm in the hospital talking to somebody who's just lost a child, I've got no more than 10 seconds' and probably five seconds' concentration level when they're going to be actually listening to me and probably rather less.

Elijah doesn't try to justify what has happened, which is very significant. He takes the child in his arms, presumably because that was what he felt God was telling him to do. For us, the action that compassion leads to, is precisely the same. It's what we feel with the Spirit of God whispering in our ear, and what we feel with our common sense is the best thing to do in the circumstances. Often the best thing you can do is give a good hug and cry with them. Not to say a word but to hug them – using your discretion – and to express complete solidarity and involvement with that person.

You could take them a meal. They may not want your company but compassion is always saying, "I'm there if you need me and I'm not going to impose myself on you, but I need you to know that I'm here. I'll do anything that is helpful." So it's a hug, it's a meal, possibly a telephone call, a letter. It's including them in whatever you're doing. And it's doing it over a period.

Usually in the case of bereavement, there's a flurry of activity in the first months or so after the death. However it is the period, three months to a year thereafter when the pain is no less and when everything is just the same, that this practical side of things needs to continue. It is relatively easy to do it for a little bit, but we need to keep going with it.

If the first response of compassion is action, the second is prayer. Elijah takes the child in his arms up to the room where he is staying, lays him on his bed and then he cries out to the Lord. I'm sure there are tears rolling down his face because this is deeply painful. "Oh Lord my God, have you brought tragedy also upon this widow I am staying with, by causing her son to die?"

The first thing I note is, there is a recognition of the reality of what's going on – this is a tragedy. As Christians, don't let's anaesthetise ourselves from these ghastly realities of life. The compassionate person will see it very vividly. The Nigerian man who lost his children doesn't want to deny the reality, and the compassionate person, the person praying, will address that to God. That's the place it should be articulated – to God.

The prayer starts off with the reality of the earthly circumstances, not blunting that at all but then going on to the character of God. "Have you brought tragedy also upon this widow I'm staying with, by causing her son to die?" which I read as, "No, you haven't." It's an element of, "You can't have done this, God!" "The God I know doesn't behave like this," is what Elijah is saying. "You're not like that." Elijah knew the character of God and that God could be trusted. He is proclaiming the truth of who God is.

It is important that we speak the reality of who God is – that he's not the God of death. He doesn't bring disasters to make life miserable. But he is the God who can be trusted and the God of love. The fact that these things happen is very much a feature of living in a fallen world, where things are very unfair, very hurtful and very cruel. There is a real power of evil that is around which, if we ignore it, means we don't get the full picture. God is not the originator of any of these things.

"I cried very briefly at the cremation but don't remember crying again for the next 14 years."

Nick and Jane Oundjian *tell the story of the tragic death of their 13-month-old son, 17 years ago*

JANE'S STORY

When my mother died 31 years ago, she had been ill for a long time. I remember she was on morphine and so wasn't conscious much of the time. But we didn't go and sit and talk with her at all. She was simply upstairs in her room and when she died, I remember creeping upstairs and peeping through the door feeling that I was doing something wrong. We didn't touch her, speak to her or hold her hand. When the undertakers came to the house, we shut ourselves in the kitchen and listened to music on the radio while she was taken away. I cried briefly at the cremation but don't remember crying again for the next 14 years.

That is an extraordinary thing and hopefully, something that would not be allowed to happen now. What effectively happened was that I was living with a dormant volcano inside me – I thought it was extinct and I had dealt with it. But of course, the eruption came with the next loss. Nick and I were childless for 10 years before we had Jeremy. He was a completely healthy child, thriving and full of beans.

When Jeremy was 13 months old, Nick went to India and Pakistan on a month's business trip. He suggested that I take Jeremy to stay with my best friend, Jeremy's godmother, in Connecticut, USA. While we were staying there, he caught what we thought was a gastroenteritis bug from a little boy of the same age. The other children in the area all had it and got better. Within a week, Jeremy had died of it. After I had nursed him for two nights, he was taken to hospital and I was persuaded to go home for the night. I did and arrived back at about seven the next morning. It turned out to be about 20 minutes after he had died. Nobody asked if I'd like to see him and I didn't think to ask – I never saw him again. It was appalling. Whilst nobody said to me he would have lived if I had stayed, I've had guilt about that for the last 17 years. I've talked about it endlessly and I don't think it will ever go away.

I also think it's a little easier to accept if you know why someone has died. Either Jeremy was that one in 5,000 who die of gastroenteritis or maybe he picked up some other branch of the virus. The unsatisfying thing for us afterwards was that although tests were done to find out what actually happened, we never got any concrete answers. These two experiences are why I'm so keen on good bereavement care.

For the first weeks after Jeremy died, all I talked about was my mother – my grief had lain buried all those years. People on the outside often want to put a time limit on bereavement. About three months after Jeremy died, a very good family friend came and said that he would like to talk to us. He said that it was the opinion of everybody that enough was enough, and we should be putting all that away now and getting on with life. I think that what he was really saying was that he couldn't cope with any more of it. This I understand. People outside just don't know how to cope. But we shouldn't be saying to bereaved people, "Enough is enough." It may be something that goes on for years and years. The guilt doesn't always disappear. It is quite common that we get left with some of it.

"Grieving is a very painful process. Some people take a very long time and don't do it very well. That was me."

NICK'S STORY

I was in Karachi when I received the news. I phoned up and Jane's best friend said, "There has been an accident." At the time I was an extremely strong and confident guy and I thought I could cope. I knew it would be all right. I'd get on the next plane, be in New York and sort it out. Then she told me that Jeremy was dead. It was 1AM and I went out and ran down the streets of Karachi in the dark. I somehow managed to get to the airport and took the first plane home. I spent nine hours underneath a blanket quietly crying.

Once I got home I felt an incredible amount of guilt that I hadn't been with them. I was absolutely convinced that it wouldn't have happened if I had been there. Stupid, of course! Every time the telephone rang during the next weeks, I was absolutely certain of Jeremy's return. They had found him. He was fine. Or when the door bell rang, I knew that there would be somebody there holding him. Of course there wasn't. As I went out to the shops, I would look in every pushchair. I was sure that he was around. This was in the immediate period after he had died. I was angry for years.

There was also confusion and helplessness. Jane would say, "Could you go to the corner shop and get a box of Bran Flakes." There is nothing easier, but I would spend 40 minutes in there deciding whether I should get ordinary Bran Flakes or Kelloggs Bran Flakes. I still remember that Kelloggs Bran Flakes were 73p and the other one was 58p. It stuck in my mind. It was such a problem for me trying to decide that.

What really made things better for us were simple things. Two or three weeks after his death, I was out walking and saw two people watching television in a shop window. They were watching a running race. I happen to love running and I watched Steve Ovett on his third lap of 1,500m. I was miserable but I was thinking, "Is he going to win it?" and he won. Then suddenly I got miserable again and I thought to myself, "Hello, I've just had 90 seconds of pleasure." That was so amazing and important. A friend of ours turned up at our door every day for six months. She had decided to come every day to our house and prevent us from being miserable the whole time. That was amazing.

The biggest contribution to my healing was going running. From the age of 12, I had gone running each day. Quite soon after losing Jeremy, I went to Battersea Park every morning and I would pound the ground and cry out in anger, tears coming down my cheeks. One day, a friend said, "I might come running with you." He had never run before and hated it. He got better at it and, after about two months, we began to talk and I would get things out. After about four months, things were improving and by the end of the year he was a better runner than me! This whole relationship was incredible because I began to realise that what he needed was to work through and grieve the loss of his father during his early adolescence. Four or five years later, he lost his son so I was able to help him work through that as well. We ran together for 12-14 years. What he did by coming out and giving himself was fantastic and possibly the greatest single contributing factor to my recovery.

Grieving is a very painful process. Some people take a very long time and don't do it very well. That was me.

"They must be allowed to be sad."

Jane Oundjian *on the importance of bereavement care*

It is helpful to remember that bereavement is not just about death. It is to do with loss, deprivation – having to do without something upon which we had been counting. It is also a loss of future hopes. These losses can include: death, divorce, disability – maybe loss of limb, sight or hearing later in life – miscarriage, abortion, redundancy, abuse and the consequent loss of childhood and innocence, rape, or in fact anything which seriously changes our perception of ourselves and our ability to function as we did.

It is absolutely biblical to grieve. There are two sides to the Christian response to bereavement. Both are very important. The first is that we know and believe that we have a bright future and that those we love who are Christians, will have gone on to everlasting life. Death for us is a continuation of our relationship with Jesus. Secondly, Jesus wept at the death of Lazarus. Jesus acknowledged and recognised what death meant for us. It is absolutely biblical to grieve. Throughout the Old and New Testaments, there are people who grieve and mourn and are encouraged to do so. It is very important that our faith isn't used like a sticking plaster to put over an unsightly and uncomfortable wound. Our faith should be used like a bowl of warm salt water and we should be bathing our wound in it. It will sting and it will hurt but it will be cleansed, purified and healed once and for all.

There are, however questions that come up for Christians: "Why me? Why should my child die? Why do I have cancer? Couldn't God have intervened to prevent this?" I think sometimes in Christian circles, a trite answer can be given by someone meaning well, like: "I'm sure God knows what this is going to bring for you." This kind of answer is given in kindness but actually conveys that the person doesn't understand the agony of the question, because it is a question that can't be answered. That doesn't mean that it must not be asked. There is also the question, "Where is God in all that's happened? I gave him everything. I became a Christian. Is he punishing me? What am I meant to be learning?"

Another very big question concerns where the person has gone, particularly if we weren't sure where they stood in relation to faith. That's a difficult one to answer. The first thing I would say is: we don't know for sure the state of anyone else's heart, right up to the last moment. We must never forget the parable of the workers in the vineyard in Matthew 20. The man paying the workers says, "I want to give the man who was hired last the same as I gave you." People really do have until the very last moment to get right with God. I think that is what he wants for them because he is a generous God.

My mother died 31 years ago and I often worried about where she might be. Two years ago, I learnt that three years before she died she went to a Billy Graham meeting in London and she went forward. For 29 years, I never knew that and I might never have found out.

Another example is Ian McCormack, a young man who was swimming somewhere in some exotic islands and was stung five times by poisonous jellyfish. Amazingly, he managed to get to shore. He was not a Christian but when he was in the ambulance he remembered what his mother had said to him: "If ever you are in trouble you must turn to the Lord Jesus and he'll forgive you." He recited the Lord's Prayer in the ambulance and when he got to the line 'Forgive us our trespasses' he remembered two people he had not forgiven. So he forgave them and finished the prayer. He survived. But he might have died and no-one, not even his mother who had prayed for him for all those years, would have known for sure. We think we're sure about people because we've known them for a long time but actually, we don't know their heart. So that's one thing that we must hold on to. Another point is that we do know that God is absolutely fair and we can never be more fair than he is.

Another burden for Christian people is the feeling, "I should be coping better than somebody who's not a Christian." I think that's an unfair burden to carry. In the end there will probably be a wonderful fruit, but it's not going to be like that right from the beginning. That's not realistic. As Christians, we must be prepared to accept unconditionally the way that our bereaved friend or relative is feeling. We must be able to cope with their sadness. They must be allowed to be sad. Often, it is a question of just being with them – sitting with them, crying with them. We must not always feel we must make it better. The bereaved person is probably longing to talk – they can't tell their story enough times. People need to talk. We can also help them by accompanying them to church, meeting them beforehand so it's not intimidating. Pray with them on a regular basis and tell them, "Two or three of us are going to pray for you."

However, the first thing is that they need a lot of practical help – washing, ironing, shopping. Going into places to buy food is daunting if you're in the first stages of grief. Say something like, "Couldn't I come in one day and do a bit of your ironing with you – I love ironing." It's just a huge help. They may want you to do something a few times and then suddenly, the fourth time they say, "No thank you" and you may feel very rejected. You have just got to take a deep breath and realise that it was the wrong moment. Try not to be too timid to go back again a week later and ask how it's going. We've got to try to bury our sensitivity. If people are having a bad day they might be quite abrupt.

When you know someone who has been bereaved, do write them a letter. Often there is an inhibition. "I'd like to write," you think, "but I didn't know them very well," or "I'm not quite sure what I would say." It's worth writing it though. I hear people saying over and over again, "The letters are so wonderful and I've kept them and I read them over again and again." You hear people saying, "I didn't know that so many people thought so much of him." So I would say if anything prompts you to write, to pick up the phone, to cross over the road or to drop in and see someone – do it, risk it!

"Every Christian is a Simon of Cyrene, voluntarily taking up the cross and following Christ."

John Collins *on 'our little crosses'*

> If anyone would come after me, he must deny himself and take up his cross and follow me. (Mark 8:34)

Immediately after scourging, it was the practice of the Romans to lay the cross beam on a condemned man's shoulders, and rope it there. This must have been appallingly painful. Then he would be led a long way round the streets of Jerusalem, for about a mile and a quarter, so that everybody could have a public display of what happened to those who disobeyed Rome. That is what it meant to take up the cross. So it is a very sombre picture when Jesus said, "Take up your cross and follow me."

At the least, it seems to me, it must involve an open following of Christ, in our work or wherever we are, on Monday, Tuesday, Wednesday, just as much as on Sunday – fully recognising that inevitably this will bring us pain. It will bring opposition, misunderstanding, dislike, contempt, and being passed over. It will bring injustice, persecution and in some parts of the world it will bring death. Traditionally, all the apostles apart from Judas and John were martyrs. Today one doesn't have to explain what it means to take up the cross in such countries as China, Ethiopia, Turkey, Malaysia, Bangladesh or the Sudan. In 1993 Bernard Levin wrote an article in The Times in which he described incidents of crucifixion – the real thing – by Islamic soldiers of Christians in Sudan today.

Even in this country, Christians are increasingly facing all sorts of subtle pressures from many factions of society – in schools, industry, the media. Listen to this:

> One of the hardest things for me just now is to accept the strain of the battle and the way it is showing in my face and is telling on my health. I suppose I've aged 10 years in the last three. This is the cross – to realise there is no glamour, no appreciation to be asked or expected; nothing but ridicule, pain and loss. But it is in this that one finds Christ.

Who was this? An ordinary Christian housewife and mother. One day God said to her, "Will you do something about pornography and violence on television?" It was Mary Whitehouse.[1]

When the pain comes, do we sit down and cry? Do we complain? Do we say, "I didn't think the Christian life was going to be like this?" No, in this we find Christ, and enter into the fellowship of his sufferings.

In the Book of Acts, when the disciples were beaten and flogged by the rulers of the synagogue, they rejoiced that they were worthy to suffer with Christ. It has been well said that every Christian is a Barabbas. We look up at the cross and say,

[1] Extract from her book, *Who Does She Think She is?*

"I ought to be there, but you have set me free." But also out of love and gratitude for what Christ has done, every Christian is a Simon of Cyrene, voluntarily taking up the cross and following Christ. Jesus asks "a cross for a cross". He invites us to take up our little crosses in response to his great cross. The irony is that those who lose their lives in this way for Christ and the gospel are the people who are fulfilled. They are the people who realise their potential. They are the people who become strong.

"Jesus, as he prayed to God the Father said, 'Father, is there another way?' and God the Father said, 'No. The only way is the cross.'"

Paul Negrut *on how God answered the prayers of Romania*

When we celebrate Christmas in Romania, we have a small Christmas tree with tiny boxes underneath. It is a special time for our children when the whole family stands around the tree and they are allowed to open those boxes. You should see their expectations as night comes. Their whole minds and personalities are under the tree. If Mum and Dad say, "Kids, it's time to go to sleep," and send them to bed, do you think they will go to sleep? They can't unless they open the boxes. They know that Mum and Dad will have something new for them – some new toy or gift, and they are so excited to see what is there.

Do you expect something from God this morning? Do you have expectations? Do you expect God to answer, to speak to you, to do something that is new and unique? Jesus said to his disciples, "Come and stay and watch with me!" Now when you stay and watch, you expect something to happen. But the disciples didn't have expectations.

I grew up in a Communist country and I remember decades of expectation as I saw churches being pulled down, pastors and church leaders arrested and killed, people being humiliated; I saw the Bible, the word of God, being confiscated, burnt or turned into toilet paper; I saw the name of God being denied or openly mocked and despised in those nations. I remember the churches looking up to heaven and expecting God to intervene. They were long decades of darkness and the church was crying out, expecting God to intervene. We met by night. We were not allowed to have prayer groups or Bible study groups. We were not allowed to bring up our children in the fear of the Lord. They were taken from us and trained in atheistic schools. But even then we had expectations.

Whenever we have expectation, God will not fail us. He is going to answer. Peter, John and James thought that the night was just an average night when Jesus said, "Stay and watch and pray!" Sometimes you feel that when you pray there is no answer. In 1974, my church started to pray that God would bring Romania times of revival, that he would open the doors for the gospel. We prayed that the gospel would be preached in Romania in stadiums, on radio and television, in newspapers and that it would be proclaimed in the parliament. People thought that we were crazy. Do you know, in 1990 those prayers were answered. We prayed in 1974 and received the answer in 1990!

Every morning at 5 o'clock, my church meets for prayer. It started in a very interesting way: an old lady about 85 years of age came one day to one of the pastors of the church and said, "Pastor, can we have a little room here in the church to pray every morning at 5 o'clock? I feel that God wants me spend the rest of my life in prayer and I have a small prayer group who want to meet every morning. We are old ladies and we want to give those morning hours to God for prayer." So the pastor said, "Yes, of course you can have a room here." That lady came with five others and they started to pray. Two days later, the pastor was very curious about what was happening there so he went to see. As soon as he stepped into that room, he felt that he should stay there. After the pastor joined that prayer group, other people heard and the group started to grow. The group grew to 20, 30, 40; there was no more room in that office for them so they moved. Now, every morning we have 400 to 500 people meeting for prayer.

In Romania, we all pray with a loud voice, not at the same time, but one at a time. We all pray and each one participates in each prayer. How can we do that? We know that God loves paragraphs but specially he loves short sentences so we pray with short sentences. One starts and says, "We pray Lord this morning that the gospel will be proclaimed on radio." Another prays for television and another for newspaper, another for the army and it builds up a prayer.

Secondly, Jesus encouraged his disciples to understand the time. This is an hour when there are so many forces of darkness marching towards eastern Europe. It is time to pray. Pornography, drugs, prostitution, all kinds of crimes, the filthiness of the Western world is moving towards those countries. It's time to pray that God will spare and save those nations that were in bondage for so many decades. This is the hour God gave to the nations in eastern Europe to hear the gospel. This is the hour to start orphanages, schools, medical centres, universities, to penetrate every single social group with the word of God. On that night when Jesus prayed in the Garden of Gethsemane, he understood that that was the great hour of salvation. It was a great hour but then Jesus, as he prayed to God the Father said, "Father, is there another way?"

and God the Father said, "No. The only way is the cross."

When you respond to God's call, you expect great things but then there is a price to be paid. Is there a way for us to serve God without paying that price? No, there is no way but do you know that we do not pay the price for salvation? We are paying the price for promulgation. Jesus paid the price for salvation. Our price is just to spread the good news.

In Romania in the days of the Communist regime, it could cost you years in jail to spread the gospel. Whenever Jesus calls us, there is a price to be paid. Are you willing to pay the price? To go to the former Soviet Union to proclaim the gospel, there is a price to be paid. To go to Romania, there is a price to be paid. To go to downtown London to spread the gospel to others, there is a price to be paid. To be faithful, there is a price to be paid. But the one who pays the price is the one who will get the crown.

"He saw that I was angry and said, 'Paul, we are not here to complain. We are here to praise our Lord. Let's kneel down and pray.'"

Paul Negrut *on what one persecuted Christian taught him*

I will tell you a story of a man who spent 17 years in Communist prisons for spreading the gospel. He was tortured every day. Sometimes he was put in the sewage of the prison. And then he was placed in the courtyard and all the other prisoners would come in and spit on him and kick him and he was asked to give up Christ. Each time after being tortured he would go into his room and write a poem and a song for Jesus. Those songs came out and now they are in a book that circulates through the churches. There are more than 800 songs he wrote in jail.

When I was in a military concentration camp, I went through times of persecution and one day I was so discouraged I was despairing. That evening the officer in charge called me and I didn't know what he wanted with me. He said to me, "Negrut, are you a Christian?" Of course he knew that I was a Christian. I was there for that reason. I said, "Yes sir, I am a Christian." He pulled me closer and said, "Paul, my parents are Christians but nobody knows. This is the secret of my life. If my bosses find out that I am from a Christian family, they are going to dismiss me or maybe kill me. Then he said, "Paul, I am the only officer in charge tonight. There is nobody around. I am the only one watching over the camp. I can give you two hours of freedom. Go somewhere." Two hours of freedom from a concentration camp! Where was I to go? He said, "If you are not back in two hours and somebody comes to inspect the camp and you are not here, you know that they will shoot me."

I remembered this man who had spent 17 years in jail and overcome torture and hatred, who lived just a few miles away over a hill. So I ran to that man's house expecting to see a shining face, to see a man that would be like an angel who would comfort me, strengthen me. I ran to his house and I opened the door, and it was not a shining face but a bleeding face. There were open scars and blood was coming down his face. I asked him what had happened and he said, "The secret police have just left my house. They searched the house and they smashed me."

I was so angry, and he saw that I was angry and said, "Paul, we are not here to complain. We are here to praise our Lord. Let's kneel down and pray." I remember that I knelt down with him but I didn't have a prayer that night. I said very few words.

John Wimber

Sandy Millar

Bishop Lesslie Newbigin

David Parker

Pastor David Yonggi Cho

Richard Foster

Jeremy Jennings

Paul Negrut

Ken Costa

Nick and Jane Oundjian

Jackie Pullinger-To

Chris Woods

Michael Cassidy

Steve Chalke

Gordon Fee

J. John

Then that man started to pray and he prayed with such fervour, excitement and love. He prayed for his enemies, he prayed for the Communists, for the secret police. He asked God's blessings over them; he asked God's forgiveness; he asked God's love to flow over their families. I opened my eyes to see if that man was normal. I never heard somebody praying for his enemies with such love as that man. After that prayer he spoke to me and said, "Paul, they come twice every week to torture me, and whenever they torture me I look straight into the eyes of the secret policeman and I say to him, "Sir, I love you. I want you to know that I love you." Then he said, "I tell him, 'Sir, if we see each other before the throne of judgement, I want you to know that I love you. But sir, if you will be eternally lost, I want you to know that you will not be there because I hate you. You'll be there because you rejected Jesus's love and my love. Sir, I love you."

One night that officer came to this man's house and the officer said to him, "Sir, I didn't come tonight to beat you. I came tonight to let you know that we will see each other before the throne of judgement." Then he said, "Sir, we will be on the same side." He said, "Brother, your love melted my heart and through your love I saw Jesus's love, and I came to know Jesus." Then he said, "I have only a few more weeks to live. The doctors have discovered that I have cancer. Within a few weeks I am going home but, before I see Jesus, I came to ask your forgiveness. I came to pray with you. I came to be reconciled with you." They prayed together. Can you see the torturer and the one tortured praying together? The officer disappeared and a few weeks later he was gone. This man endured the torture, paid the price and said I love you. Aren't you glad that Jesus paid the price? He went to the cross and gave his life. We are saved and we will see him face to face.

"'Can somebody sing here?' he asked himself. 'Can somebody praise God and say, "What a foretaste of glory divine" in this hell?'"

Paul Negrut *gives an illustration of faith in solitary confinement*

Let me tell you about one man who was sentenced for many decades. He spent years in solitary confinement and he didn't know if it was day or night. He had no understanding of time. Was it winter or summer? He was totally out of time and space, in darkness all alone. One day or night, he felt a prompting of the Holy Spirit to sing a song. Now if you are in a Communist prison, and you sing a song, that's death for sure. But he couldn't resist. There was that kind of prompt, that push of the Spirit. So he began to sing: "Blessed Assurance, Jesus is mine. Oh what a foretaste of glory divine. This is my story, this is my song, praising my Saviour, all the day long!" And he sang and he rejoiced.

In the next room, in darkness, was another prisoner, a non-Christian. That man was in the middle of a psychological breakdown. He had decided he couldn't live any more and would commit suicide. So he had taken his shirt and made a rope and hanged himself from one of the iron bars in the prison. He was hanging there to die when he heard his neighbour singing, "Blessed Assurance, Jesus is mine. Oh what a foretaste of glory divine." He was amazed. "Can somebody sing here?" he asked himself. "Can somebody praise God and say, 'What a foretaste of glory divine' in this hell?" The man said, "I have to live and find out!" So he loosened himself.

Months later, they were both taken out and were given dirty jobs in the prison just to keep the humiliation and persecution going. The Christian was asked to polish all the stones in the courtyard of the prison with his palms until they were shining. So he was polishing them, bleeding and hurting. The other one was asked to do another dirty job some yards away from him. They didn't know each other. As they were there, the Christian again felt the prompting that he should sing this song but now he was a little afraid. You see, in the courtyard even if he was still a prisoner and persecuted, it was a little better than in the solitary confinement. So he was afraid that if he sang the song he would be sent back there. Can you identify that feeling when you know that you have to do something but you are hesitant, and you look for a compromise? You cannot say a definite no but you do not want to say a definite yes.

Finally he came up with a creative alternative – he would whistle the song. As he whistled, the other heard the tune and he recognised it and forgetting about everything – prison, persecution, punishment and terror – he approached this man and said, "Do you know this song?" and the man said, "Yes." The other said, "Tell me, were you in that wing of the solitary confinement?" and the Christian replied, "Yes." The man said, "Did you sing that song there?" and the Christian said, "Yes, I did," and the man said, "Thank you for saving my life. I was hanging there, committing suicide when I heard you singing this song, I decided to leave and find out. Tell me!"

The other one shared Christ with him there and the non-Christian accepted Christ. The new kingdom of God began to grow in prison. There are many stories I can tell you like that.

"Great things start with great decisions."

Paul Negrut *on being ready to die for Christ*

How do you live your life in the world but not as the world? First of all, who is your master? We live in a world where it is popular to do whatever you want. The Bible says no. We are servants. God from eternity took upon himself the image of a servant. When Christ came to teach us how to live in the world, he taught us the lesson of servanthood. Do you know the only right a servant has? The only right is that of perfect obedience.

Does somebody claim total authority over my life? Yes, God does. Jesus says, "Unless you deny everything, take your cross and follow me, you are not worthy." When we speak about Christianity and when you live in a Communist country, Christianity is not, "Let's see. We will decide tomorrow." Christianity is, "I am ready to die for Christ." If you are ready to die for him, you are ready to live for him. If you are not ready to die, you are not ready to live.

Daniel was ready to die. When he said, "I'm not going to defile myself," he put himself in the place of death. He said, "I am ready to die. I belong to God so completely that I am ready to die, I am not going to turn away from God." An army general came from the war and was interviewed by the press. A journalist said, "What was the number one cause of casualties in the war?" The general said, "The number one cause of casualties in our ground war was that our soldiers didn't take decisions once and for all before they entered the war. My greatest problem was to teach my soldiers to take decisions once and for all. They went to war assuming that in every situation they would evaluate the circumstances and they would decide according to those circumstances. As they were trying to figure out the things they might do, the enemy shot them because the enemy had already taken the decision. My soldiers looked at the enemy wondering, "Should I or should I not kill him?" They died. If we'd had soldiers who had taken decisions once and for all before they entered the war, we would have won the war with very few casualties."

Why do the churches lose so many members? Because many Christians do not take decisions once and for all. When you come to Christ, you have to take the one decision from which there is no way back: "I totally belong to him." When the man who spent 14 years in jail took that decision, he was ready. When the interrogation started, his decision was already made. Now do you have decisions to make?

We all dream of doing great things with our lives but great things start with great decisions. I worked in secular society for seven years as a clinical psychologist and in those days, I agonised because I couldn't witness to any of my colleagues because I was so much under interrogation and persecution and many other restrictions on my life. All my colleagues would run away from me because if they had been seen speaking to me, the secret police might assume there was a connection between us and they too would undergo persecution. After seven years, it seemed to me, that time was almost useless, that my life there didn't make any difference.

After the Revolution, so many of my colleagues who had refused to talk to me came to know Christ that, in the Christian University we started, the Department of Theology and Psychology/Social Work is composed of my former colleagues who refused to speak to me in those days. When they were baptised, we asked them how they came to know Jesus Christ and some of them told how they had been watching me closely in those days when we were under persecution, to see if I would compromise. They said, "We were longing that God would bring to our lives the day when we could take decisions and stand for Christ." If you live a godly life where you are, one day in your lifetime or after you have gone into eternity, you will see the difference.

"No, I will not divorce him. He is my husband and I am going to live here and he will see my love and my faith and my faithfulness until the very last day."

Paul Negrut *gives an illustration of one woman's commitment*

One of my brothers was, for a number of years, the pastor of a small village church. He had a godly lady in his church whose husband was a very wicked, ungodly man. That man was a drunkard, a wild fellow and he would beat his wife whenever he came home. Her family told her she should not live her life with this man and that she had a right to divorce him. She said, "No, I will not divorce him. He is my husband and I am going to live here, and he will see my love and my faith and my faithfulness until the very last day." Some years later, that man began to bring prostitutes home and live with prostitutes in the same house as his wife.

About the same time, she got ill with cancer and as she was lying in bed he would bring the prostitutes to the same room under the very eyes of his wife. Now by that time her family was so angry they went to take her out and said, "We want you to die in peace. You cannot die in this hell. This man is a demon." She said, "No, I will not leave this house. I married this man and I am going to live here until God will take me away. He will see that I am going into eternity in love and respect for him." And she died.

My brother led the funeral. There in the cemetery, standing over the grave and the corpse, my brother spoke to the crowd. As he did so, the husband broke in and said, "Can I speak? I killed a saint, I murdered a godly woman. Is there forgiveness for me under the sun?" He fell down near the coffin; my brother stopped the procession and approached this man and witnessed Christ to him. The man accepted Christ there on the graveside and now he is an active member in that church! The whole village is now coming to church to see the miracle of God and you can trace the miracle back to that woman who took a very strong decision.

You say, "Is God fair to me?" Well, let me ask you, "Was God fair to Christ? Was God fair to let him die for us? If you say God was unfair to Christ, you can say God is unfair to you. But my question is, "Was there another way for salvation?" There is a great glory for God when you are in the world but not as the world.

"Whenever you have nothing, that's the greatest starting point. Nothing is raw material for God!"

Paul Negrut *tells the story of an unusual Lord's Supper in prison*

In the early 1950s when the Communists arrested all the religious leaders and imprisoned them to destroy Christianity, initially they scattered them in different parts of the world so they would not be two Christians in one place. They would be isolated and alone. However, several years later, the Communists got together a group of Christian leaders in one prison cell. One Sunday morning, after about seven years of being tortured and persecuted, they saw each other and it was such a joy that they decided to celebrate. It was Easter Day and they asked what should they do to celebrate their gathering together.

One of them said, "Let's celebrate the Lord's Supper." Another of them said, "It's a great idea but we have nothing to celebrate the Lord's Supper with. Why don't we wait until we have something?" Richard Wurmbrand, who was among them said, "No, we cannot postpone it. We never know if we will have another time to celebrate. Let's celebrate the Lord's Supper with nothing." So one of them took nothing, he blessed nothing, he broke nothing and he shared nothing with each one of them. They ate nothing but remembered the body of Christ. Then another one took nothing, blessed nothing, poured to each of them nothing, they drank nothing and they remembered the blood of Jesus. The glory of God came into that room and they were filled with power, and with the assurance that God was there, he was alive and the Spirit was there. They were so joyful.

That afternoon, they were scattered and for seven years none of them saw another Christian. When they came out from prison, Richard told me this story and said, "Paul, we learnt in prison this lesson – whenever you have nothing, that's the greatest starting point. Nothing is raw material for God! He created the whole universe out of nothing."

He said, "Whenever you have nothing, it is a new beginning of creation. If you wait until you have something, you will never start. If you wait until you have a car, you will not be good enough. If you wait for 10 million pounds, there is a recession and you will need 20 million pounds. If you have nothing, give it to God. This is how we work in Romania."

"When you stand before him you'll know it was just and fair, and merciful and loving because that's his nature. It's his character."

John Wimber *reflects on eternal life and a conversation he had with Patrick Pearson Miles, a young man suffering from a severe kidney disease*

I want to talk about eternal life in the context of a couple of exchanges I had. One of them occurred during lunch with a number of Vineyard leaders from England. It was a mixed group and one of the older guys said to me, "How are you feeling these days?" I said, "Well, just full of gratitude. I am so grateful for the blessings of God in my life."

One of the younger, newer people said to me, "What do you mean?"

I said, "All of my children love the Lord and have all married spouses that love the Lord. They're raising their children in the Lord. They love the church. They love the cause of God. Nothing would make a person more devastated than to have children who didn't love the Lord. Frankly, everything else that comes along as a blessing or success, is a bonus."

As we were leaving the place this same person said to me, "How does that match up with your recent stroke and your cancer, and your heart attack a long time ago?" I thought, "Oh no, here we go again." I said, "It matches up perfectly because I am not that focused on this life. I gave it up when I became a Christian. I realise that this is a little different to what is preached by a lot of people but it's the very essence of what I understand to be Christianity. When I came to Jesus I gave up my sin but I also gave up my life. He gave me a new life – eternal life that would extend beyond this carcass."

What we get in this life is a gift from God – and the main purpose of this life is to discover that gift. I spent 29 years not knowing that it existed. Then we encountered somebody who told me all about it. One night I received Jesus. I prayed and he received me because from that day until this – which is over 31 years – it's been good. There have been bumps – you know like speed bumps – every now and then that have happened in life but there is nothing that hasn't been in his hands and in his control. There is nothing that has taken the quality of life away from me.

From time to time, I have talked to brothers and sisters who have had a difficulty. They've lost a husband or wife. They've lost a child. They've had great pain in life. I am not making light of that but I just can't feel all that bad, particularly when they've lost them to Jesus. I recognise that it is hard to live alone – the sheets are cold and no-one else is in the room and you have to make your way with a new kind of focus.

Paul writes: "Paul, a servant of God and an apostle of Jesus Christ for the faith of God's elect and the knowledge of the truth that leads to godliness – a faith and knowledge resting on the hope of eternal life, which God, who does not lie, promised before the beginning of time."(Titus 1:1-2) He is an apostle with a purpose and that purpose is to preach eternal life. I believe that all of the church has been called to this preaching. All of the church is to prophesy the life that's in Christ. We are to do it to anyone that will stand still long enough to hear us. It is, 'a faith and knowledge resting on the hope of eternal life, which God, who does not lie, promised before the beginning of time.' I think it is really important that you have that underlined in your Bible. For God, *who does not lie*. You see one of the principle challenges of the enemy from beginning to end is, "Hath God said?" It brings into question the veracity of

God. Has God said? Can you trust God? Can you trust what
God says? When Satan spoke with Jesus, one of the
underlining issues was, "If you are the son of God, then do this
etc." Again, veracity, truthfulness, integrity – these are always
attacked by the enemy. Obliquely, he will do the same things to
you.

During the first trip after my recovery from cancer, Sandy
Millar asked me to speak at Holy Trinity Brompton and he
invited me to lunch afterwards. A handsome young man came
in who I could see was quite ill. He sat with me and we talked
for about two hours. When he began sharing his story with me,
it became apparent to me that he was quite desperate to be
healed. He was dying of kidney failure and it had been a long
journey of about ten years through various stages of the
problem. He was very focused on healing and he had sort of a
'if God does not heal me, I cannot believe there is a God' kind
of mentality.

He was aware of my cancer and knew that if I were to get it
again, it would occur in the next two months and that unlike a
lot of other cancers, the type I had usually re-occurs within the
first two years of treatment and I was coming up to the first two
years. I had my first examination and they did not find any
cancer in my body at this time. I'm glad for that but the truth is,
it could still re-occur any time. But I am not laying awake at
night worrying about cancer. I believe a song we used to sing,
"He has the whole world in his hands," – it's simple but
profound. It's all in his hands and we can trust him.

The guy and his wife blinked at me. I said, "Do you save
milk cartons?" They said, "Well no, when the milk's gone we
discard them," and I said, "How about bread wrappers. Do you
save those?" They said, "We throw them away after the bread's
used." So I said, "Well, isn't that what you're going to do with
this life? Why are you clinging to it so much? The value was
never in the carton or the wrapper. It was always in that which
it contained."

I am going to touch on some of the highlights of an article about the young man I met at HTB – an article published in that church's newspaper, *Focus*, some months after our talk – because I think it is important you understand the way he viewed things at one time, and the way he viewed them after our meeting.

Here he describes the condition – it's called Nephritic Syndrome – and he said:

They think I got the disease from a throat infection, literally a sore throat. Apparently, a bug gets in through the throat and perforates the kidneys and the protein in the blood stream then flows out through the holes. When we were initially told about my illness, it was quite a shock and I prayed then and I have prayed nearly every day since then for healing.

As I have said, the day I spoke with him he was very fixed on healing and very desperate. It is one thing if you are 75, 80, 85 or 90 and you are desperate to cling to life. This young man would have been around 30. I have children that age and I felt very compassionate towards him. I also felt the need to instruct him that he had already received the more important gift in life and that was salvation, the gift of life that comes in Jesus. If God chose to give him healing, well the more the blessing, but if he chose not to, God had not failed him nor had he failed God. It was perfectly all right to ask. It was perfectly all right to pursue healing.

I was happy to pray for him that day. He asked me to and I did but I said, "I have no revelation in my heart that God is going to heal you at this point but I am happy to just pray for you and ask God that he will heal you." But the point I was trying to make for the young man – and we laughed together – was, "It's all God. We can ask, but it's all up to him and if he chooses not to give it to you, he'll answer for himself. When you stand before him you'll know it was just and fair, and

merciful and loving because that's his nature. It's his character." The young man was not really conscious of that so we
talked at length that day about this greater gift.

At another point in his story, he said,

> I had always said that if my kidneys packed up, I was not keen to
> go on dialysis. I didn't fancy the idea of that and my mum had
> always said that if she matched, she would give me one of her
> kidneys. So it was decided that we would go for a transplant from
> my mother. This is after about eight or nine years of various kinds
> of treatments all of which were exhausted. The doctors were no
> longer recommending anything else. The only thing they could do
> was a transplant. We had a number of matching tests and one was
> not a good match for some reason, and another was good and the
> last one was borderline. As the testings were uneven, the surgeons
> were hesitating. They wanted for each test to come back strong and
> say,"Yes, this kidney will survive in that body." And so they were
> slightly apprehensive about doing the transplant but kidney
> transplants from live donors have a very good record of working
> and particularly from relatives. So they went ahead and took the
> chance. But as it turned out the kidney failed.

At the time I met him, he had just found that out about six
weeks earlier. He had begun dialysis which was for him the
worst thing that could happen. It was in a sense worse than
dying because he had resisted it for so long. He says:

> In about May 1994, they made the decision to remove the kidney
> because it was killing me. They discovered that it was riddled with
> the original disease which was extremely unusual. The disease
> would normally take at least five years if it did come back. Mine
> had taken two months. The whole period was really difficult and
> the doctor told me afterwards that in his opinion, I nearly died on
> three different occasions. They decided not to tell me and
> afterwards I was glad because, I was having a hard enough time
> with just what I knew.

Partially, this is what I have called 'clinging to the container'. Again, it is not something you would blame anybody for, particularly a young man with a beautiful young wife just beginning life and wanting to succeed. But for me, it is a secondary issue. It is not the primary reason for existence. It's just that if I am going to keep on breathing and functioning, I would rather be doing it in a way that leaves me some flexibility in terms of the quality and the dignity of life. Here, he talks about himself and his wife:

> From then on, it has been a matter of getting used to life on dialysis and we have prayed a lot and nothing has gone according to plan. But at each stage that it has been very dangerous, we have been brought through. I now have a dialysis machine at home. I do just under six hours dialysis three times a week.

I don't know how many of you are familiar with dialysis but it is quite a painful process. Three times a week, he has six hours of treatment – no fun. He goes on to talk about a major change that occurred between the time he realised he was going to have to go on dialysis, and the time he did the interview which resulted in this article. He says:

> A major change in my perspective of God has happened through all of this. My faith has grown enormously. Up till now I have always been very self sufficient.

That is so much in the American ethos – this business of self sufficiency. Self reliance, self sufficiency, doing our own thing. It's so built-in. It's very difficult within our Christian understanding to yield to the power and presence of God. In fact, we have difficulty in understanding anything outside of our self sufficiency in God. But I understand the desperation of the dialysis at the time. He said:

> Although I had given my life to the Lord, I was quite happily doing

things in my own strength because I was able to and I was strong and fit.....

The implication was that he thought it was the proper way to live the Christian life. But I tell you, the Christian life is not about strength. It is about weakness. In a sense, it is weakness in us that gives revelation to his strength. In our weakness, we give ourselves to him. In our sin, in our inability to alter the course of our lives we come to Jesus. We say, "Oh Jesus, take my life. Take my sin. Take me in my weakness."

So often in my own life, I treated my conversion as a jump-start on a cold March morning with the car and then said, "Oh thanks, I'm under way now. Thanks Jesus, I'll see you up in heaven," and I was off and running. But again and again, he had to allow the battery to go down and the vehicle not to function before I got the understanding. He gave it to me in Scripture but he also gave it to me in life. It became apparent to me over the first half a dozen years that it wasn't about me getting strong. It was about the revelation of his strength in me. Though I had become quite skilled in Scripture in those years and I had memorised literally a couple of thousand texts (I had joined a Bible Memory Course) and had witnessed to a lot of friends and seen them saved – still, the truth was that when I was left to my own devices, I would always turn to sin.

Now I am not turning to the same sin – thank God. I am not turning to the same grade and quality of sin that I would have as a younger Christian. Nor am I captured in the ways that I was at different times in my spiritual pilgrimage. There have been some improvements in my record so to speak, in my walk with God. But I don't see anything of self reliance at this point in my life that is worth giving any energy to.

The father of this young man is a vicar in an Anglican Church. He is a man of about my age. He came up behind me one day, handed me a letter and kissed me on the cheek. He had tears running down his face. He said, "I am so grateful for what you did for my son." Well, I'm so grateful for what his son did with what I did. He believed it. You see it takes two to make it work.

God had to do what he did through Jesus and you have to do what you do in life – and that's receive, believe, embrace and draw him to yourself, and rely on him in every circumstance or every situation. Nobody had it any tougher than Paul. Remember when God spoke to Ananias he said, "...go and tell Paul the things he must suffer for my name's sake." (Acts 9:16). Nearly every chapter of the gospel of John deals with eternal life: "Just as Moses lifted up the snake in the desert so the Son of Man must be lifted up so that everyone who believes in him may have eternal life. For God so loved the world that he gave his one and only Son that whoever believes in him shall not perish but have eternal life..." Over and over again – eternal life, eternal life. That's what you got when you came to Jesus – eternal life. So don't cling to the wrapper or container so hard.

The mission of the Church

"Where shall wisdom be found?"

Bishop Lesslie Newbigin *on knowledge of God in public life*

There is a mine for silver and a place where gold is refined. Iron is taken from the earth, and copper is smelted from ore. Man puts an end to the darkness; he searches the farthest recesses for ore in the blackest darkness. Far from where people dwell he cuts a shaft, in places forgotten by the foot of man; far from men he dangles and sways. The earth, from which food comes, is transformed below as by fire; sapphires come from its rocks, and its dust contains nuggets of gold. No bird of prey knows that hidden path, no falcon's eye has seen it. Proud beasts do not set foot on it, and no lion prowls there. Man's hand assaults the flinty rock and lays bare the roots of the mountains. He tunnels through the rock; his eyes see all its treasures. He searches the sources of the rivers and brings hidden things to light. But where can wisdom be found? Where does understanding dwell? Man does not comprehend its worth; it cannot be found in the land of the living. The deep says, "It is not in me," the sea says, "It is not with me." It cannot be bought with the finest gold, nor can its price be weighed in silver. It cannot be bought with the gold of Ophir, with precious onyx or sapphires. Neither gold nor crystal can compare with it, nor can it be had for jewels of gold. Coral and jasper are not worthy of mention; the price of wisdom is beyond rubies. The topaz of Cush cannot compare with it; it cannot be bought with pure gold. Where then does wisdom come from? Where does understanding dwell? It is hidden from the eyes of every living thing, concealed even from the birds of the air. Destruction and Death say, "Only a rumour of it has reached our ears." God understands the way to it and he alone knows where it dwells, for he views the ends of the earth and sees everything under the heavens. When he established the force of the wind and measured out the waters, when he made a decree for the rain and a path for the thunderstorm, then he looked at wisdom and appraised it; he confirmed it and tested it. And he said to man, "The fear of the Lord – that is wisdom, and to shun evil is understanding." (Job 28)

This passage from the book of Job is a wonderful celebration of the powers of human technology. We are given a picture of men burrowing into the very heart of the mountains, opening up shafts deep in the earth, breaking the flinty rocks and smelting out of them gold, silver, copper and precious stones. Here are all the marvellous achievements of human technology beyond anything that the rest of creation can boast. However, at the end comes that haunting question, "But where shall wisdom be found?"

Doesn't that speak to our situation? We are very proud of our technology. Technology is developing at a fantastic speed, faster than ever before. We are discovering ways of doing things that we never dreamed of doing. Yet at the same time, as we celebrate our technology, we are also frightened of it. We don't know where it is leading us. It seems to create for us problems that we simply cannot solve. It's a long time since the days of the 19th and early 20th centuries, when people like H.G. Wells and many other popularisers of science were telling us that science was the real religion for the future; that science and technology would solve all our human problems and enable us to live the kind of life we want to live on earth.

Even as recently as the 1960s, we had the same burst of confidence in our technology, celebrated by John F. Kennedy on his inauguration day when he promised to put a man on the moon within a decade. Our own Harold Wilson talked about the 'white heat of the new technology' which was somehow going to raise the nation to a new level of greatness.

Today, however we are much more inclined to question where our technology is leading us. It seems as if we are not leading our technology but that it is leading us. What are we to do with the new achievements with genetic engineering? Are we really now to be made responsible for the kind of human beings we are going to allow to exist in the world? Who is wise enough to make those decisions? We seem to be led by a power that we cannot control. The former head of the European Commission, Jacques Delors, used a vivid metaphor when he said that it seems as if the world is like a plane on an automatic pilot; nobody knows where the pilot has been programmed to go and nobody knows how to unlock the pilot. We seem to be fixed on a plane headed for a destination that we do not know and cannot control. So we ask the question, "Where shall wisdom be found?"

We know the difference between cleverness and wisdom. We know the difference between the power to do what we want to do and the wisdom to know what is worth doing. I sometimes think that one of the most poignant illustrations of our dilemma is provided by our modern television. If you go and stay in a hotel in the United States, there will be a TV in your bedroom with 30 channels to choose from; if you ever waste your time trying all the channels, you will find that you have a choice of 30 different brands of rubbish. Isn't it strange that the incredible wizardry of satellite television, with all the amazing achievements of technology that make it possible, is used to deliver a cataract of trash into our homes. Where shall wisdom be found?

The same problem faces us in our political and social life. There is a constant conflict in our economic order between human needs and human wants. It often seems that our economic system is geared to satisfy any want, however crazy. Yet it leaves fundamental human needs unmet. How do you decide between needs and wants? If we were rational people, we would want what we need to bring us to our true goal, to the true end of our journey. But we are not allowed to know what the true end of our journey is. Not so long ago, every child in a Scottish school was taught, as one of the first facts to be learned, that man's chief end is to glorify God and enjoy him for ever. That is what we are made for but no education authority would allow you to teach that as a fact in a school today. That's 'just a personal opinion'. We have no public truth about what is the end for which we exist. What is the purpose of human life? Therefore what are the things that are worth desiring? What are the things worth putting our technology to serve? Where is that wisdom to be found?

We are all part of a society that has been shaped by the great change that took place roughly 300 years ago in the public life of Europe. For more than 1000 years, European thinking had been shaped by the Bible which gives us a clear picture of God's purpose for human life, a picture which is known to us by revelation through Jesus Christ. But in those terrible religious wars of the 17th century when Christians were fighting each other over their different understandings of the Bible, things changed. There was a great revulsion against the whole idea of revelation and men like John Lock, in this country, arose to say, "Look, there is a better way. Forget about these divine revelations. Nobody can be sure about them. Use your reason. Study the facts. See what is actually the case and then use your reason to relate the facts to each other so that we understand this world that we live in." That seemed so reasonable and rational that it has been the solution adopted for the last 300 years. "You can have your religious ideas if you keep them to yourself but don't bring them into the public area. Don't bring religion into politics. Don't bring ideas of divine revelation into the world of science."

However, there is one very great snag. There is a great deal that we can learn from observing the facts and using our reason but there is one thing that the use of reason and observation can never tell us. That is the purpose for which things exist. For those 1,000 years before, it had been accepted that the way to understand something was to know its purpose. But our modern world has eliminated that and believes that the way to understand something is to use observation and reason. If for example, you were someone who had never seen a clock and found a clock lying on the ground, you could use your powers of observation and reason to find out completely how it works. You could work out what causes which wheel to move, why and how far. But how would you know what it is for? Is it for decorating the sitting-room or is it for throwing at the cat? What is it for? No one can answer that question except either the designer of the clock, or someone who is accustomed to clocks and knows what they are for. When you move from studying the way it works, to asking the question, "What is it for?" you move on to a different logical level.

We could use another illustration. A neurosurgeon can examine the workings of the brain and learn how the incredibly sensitive nerves and synapses in the brain function but even the most spectacular extension of the powers of neurosurgery would not enable the surgeon to know what the man was thinking at the time. That is a completely different logical level.

That same distinction of levels runs right through all our knowledge. If there was time to do it, I could show you how the different sciences work on different logical levels. Physics deals with the basic atomic structure of things. Chemistry deals with the way the molecules combine in various ways. Chemistry depends upon physics but you cannot replace chemistry by physics. So it is with the boundary between chemistry and mechanics, or between mechanics and biology. Similarly, you cannot replace sociology or psychology, by biology. Each of these levels of learning has a distinct autonomy but not an absolute autonomy.

If that is true, then it must surely be that the highest level of all, is the level where the purpose of things finally resides –

namely, in the mind of God. That must be the highest level. Not
that theology would interfere with, or seek to control, the other
levels of learning but that none of them would be complete
without that final level. If you ask, "How can we know the
purpose for which the world exists?" the answer can only be:
"If the one whose purpose it is tells us." So to exclude divine
revelation from the field of public knowledge as Europe did
300 years ago, is to exclude the possibility of knowing whether
our life has any purpose at all.

The second consequence of that is: if you do not know the
purpose for which a thing exists, you cannot say whether it is
good or bad. You cannot use the words, 'good' or 'bad', of
anything unless you know what it is for. When I was a school-
boy, there was a big World Boy Scout Jamboree at Anfield
Park in Liverpool. Scouts from all over the world gathered. Just
about that time, there was a new product unleashed upon the
world called Shredded Wheat. One morning during that camp,
Shredded Wheat was issued to all the units for breakfast. At
10 o'clock, there was a complaint from the Nigerian Scouts:
"These pan-scrubbers are no good." If you don't know what a
thing is for, you cannot use the words, 'good' or 'bad'. If there
is no public doctrine about what a human being is for, then
there is no way by which you can say that some kind of
behaviour is 'good' and another is 'bad'. You cannot use those
words. So we don't use those words. We don't talk about good
and bad. We say, we have 'different values'. That's where we
are now.

We here, thank God, are witnesses of the fact that God has
made his purpose known. We are witnesses through what God
has done for us in Jesus Christ, to the fact that this whole world
is not a meaningless mindless machine but that it has its origins
in that glorious communion of love and joy which is the holy
Trinity – Father, Son and Holy Spirit. This whole created world
is an overflow of that love so that there might be a theatre for
God's glory. We have been put within this universe to shape it

according to God's plan in order that at the end we may share in the joy, the love and the peace of the divine being. We are here as witnesses to that fact and that is our witness to the world. Note two things about what I have said:

Firstly, when we talk about God revealing his purpose, we are not just talking about the communication of some information. As we know, it is by the costly act of the atonement wrought in Jesus Christ, that he has reconciled us from our alienation so that we cannot only know, but also love and serve the purpose for which God has created the world. We are not just talking about information. We are talking about incarnation, invitation, reconciliation, about God drawing us into his own purpose of love.

Secondly, when we speak this way, some of our contemporaries will accuse us by saying that this is just a leap of faith. "You can't show any reasons for it. It's just what you think. It's just an irrational action of faith," they say. What shall we say to that? I think we can say three things. The other day I was trying to communicate the gospel with a young man, who said, "Well, that's just what you think." I said, "Well, of course it's what I think. Can you know anything without thinking?" There is no way of knowing except by using our minds which are limited, creaturely minds. The second is that we can turn upon our questioner and say, "Tell me what you believe," and it will not be difficult to show that it rests upon commitments which cannot be proved in advance. Thirdly, this is not an irrational leap into the dark. It is the response to a personal call. It is the Lord saying to us, "Follow me" and we follow. If we imagine that there is something more reliable, more fundamental upon which we can rest our lives than what God has done for us in Jesus Christ, then one has to say that that is simply an illusion. We believe, because we have been called by the mercy of God in Jesus Christ and by the power of his Holy Spirit in his community, to bear this witness. There are no grounds upon which we can be accused of being irrational.

So here is the answer to the question, "Where shall wisdom be found?" As it is given in this chapter of Job: "The fear of the Lord is the beginning of wisdom." That means – to know the Lord, to love him, to fear him. That is wisdom. That has two consequences, one negative and one positive.

The negative consequence, as I have already hinted, is that we have to unmask, de-mythologise, all the claims to wisdom that rest upon some other foundation. The world is full of claims to knowledge, many of which are simply illusions. We have to be ready to be sceptics. People always think of sceptics as those who doubt the Christian religion. But why should that be so? I am a sceptic because I doubt an enormous amount of what is daily handed over to me on the radio and in the newspapers. I am a sceptic about an enormous amount of what is simply taken for granted in our public life. For example, that 'the main business of a nation is to increase its gross national product'. Or that 'the main purpose of human life is to express oneself and develop oneself'. There are many other things that one could mention that are nonsense but which are simply accepted as truth.

The positive thing is that we accept a calling to 'bring every thought into captivity to Christ'. We read in the letter to the Colossians, a wonderful passage about Christ as the corner-stone of the whole cosmos, the cause and the cornerstone of the world. "Christ the beginning and the end, Christ the one who holds all things together, Christ the one in whom all things shall finally be made one." To acknowledge that, sets us on a tremendous pilgrimage of re-thinking all our thoughts in whatever sphere. We're not talking here about religion. We're talking about the public life of the world – its economics, its politics, its science, its culture, its art, its music, everything. We're talking about bringing every area of human life into captivity to Christ.

Now that is a very big task. It calls for everything that we have to give. It calls for our working together with those in the same sector of public life so that we can pray together about ways in which the Lordship of Christ is to be manifested in this or that sector. It means that we do not withdraw into a private world as the secular world would like us to do, where we keep our religious beliefs to ourselves and do not allow them to get out into the public world. It means that we abandon the sort of timidity which so often makes Christians apologetic in the face of what are supposed to be the assured truths of some secular science.

It is a call to be extremely bold. It is a costly warfare because it exposes us sometimes in very dangerous situations, to the powers of this world. But, as Paul says in the letter to the Romans, "I beseech you, be not conformed to this world, but be transformed by the renewing of your minds that you may know what is the good and perfect will of God." That 'renewing of our minds' is our calling. It demands everything that we have. It demands that we help one another in doing it and it demands that we call upon all the resources of the Holy Spirit to strengthen us in our service. Therefore our whole life in the public sector will be a provisional manifestation of that glory – the glory of the triune God, the glory which is his purpose for the whole cosmos, the glory which he has revealed to us in Jesus Christ and of which he has given us a foretaste in his Holy Spirit. To him, Father, Son and Holy Spirit, be praise and glory for ever.

"He's chosen the weak because they don't have anything except Jesus."

Jackie Pullinger-To *on ministry with the poor*

All they asked was that we should continue to remember the poor, the very thing I was eager to do. (Galatians 2:10)

When, in this passage, the early church was sending Paul and Barnabas out to start a new church, they gave them one piece of advice. I'm very interested in this piece of advice. If you were sending out a team to church plant or to start a new mission somewhere, what would be the piece of advice you would give? I'm very interested to find that the piece of advice here was this: that they continue to remember the poor. Now, this is fascinating because of all the things that they could have added like, "Keep the people tithing," or "Remember prayer is most important," or "Don't forget to break bread," or whatever. The only extra advice for this couple who were going to plant where there had been no previous planting was they should remember the poor. I wonder why. What I hope to share with you is the fact that one of the reasons we are asked to remember the poor is that it is for our benefit.

You see it's a paradox. Many of us, when we think in terms of being involved with poor people or difficult people or delinquent people, imagine that it is going to cost us. Most of us feel threatened because we feel that some demand is going to be made on us which is greater than that which is going to be made on other people – therefore this ministry becomes optional. People say, "Oh, Jackie's got a mercy ministry." I don't like the term 'mercy ministry'. You see, I believe that all of us, as part of loving Jesus should be involved with the poor and that this is not optional. I believe one of the reasons this is so is that it keeps us passionately dependent upon the heart of God and that's a mercy.

I want to suggest that ministry with the poor is not an optional ministry for 'those poor people who are going to have to suffer for the rest of their life'. It's a privilege for those who will accept it and it is the greatest, because it is what Jesus did. Look at I Corinthians 1. This is what I call God's bias:

> Brothers, think of what you were when you were called. Not many of you were wise by human standards; not many were influential; not many were of noble birth. But God chose the foolish things of the world to shame the wise; God chose the weak things of the world to shame the strong. He chose the lowly things of this world and the despised things – and the things that are not – to nullify the things that are, so that no-one may boast before him. (I Corinthians 1:26-29)

He's saying to them: amongst you there are not many who've got good education by human standards, or who come from good families, or who know the right people, or who would get things done. We see from Scripture that it isn't that there won't be any well-educated people in heaven; it isn't that there won't be any who come from good families or there won't be any with influence in the world. It just says that there won't be many. The majority are going to be the others. That's another reason to minister with the poor because they are easily going to be the majority in the Kingdom of God.

In the world, we do it the other way around. We look for those that we think would influence people. We look for those that we think have leadership qualities. We pick those that look good. I see from Scripture that the Lord's done the opposite – always. He's picked the least. He's chosen the weak, the hopeless, those of no account. Why? Because they don't have anything else except Jesus. Many of us look at it like this: we say when we are praying about who might next come to the

Lord, "Wouldn't it be super if so-and-so came to the Lord. He could influence so many people."

It's not necessary. God doesn't need that kind of influence. He needs the poor in spirit because they can be filled with his. He doesn't need those who are influential in this world because they'll use their influence instead of his. He may choose to use some of those people but it will not be because of their influence. It will be despite it which is what Paul, of course, learned. And it is what he says in Philippians 3:

> If anyone ... thinks he has reasons to put confidence in the flesh, I have more: circumcised on the eighth day, of the people of Israel, of the tribe of Benjamin...; as for legalistic righteousness, faultless. But whatever was to my profit I now consider loss for the sake of Christ... I consider them rubbish, that I may gain Christ... (Philippians 3:4-8)

He says, "If anyone has reason to boast in this world I have: I went to the right school, I was in the right family, got the right qualifications, theological school, the whole bit." Then he goes on to say, "But now I consider that which was to my profit, loss for the sake of Christ. I consider them rubbish." And the word in Scripture is much ruder than rubbish. He says, "I consider all that good family, influence, education and training as..." and it's a very rude word, it's ruder than dung. When he chose to lose the importance of all those things, then God may or may not have used them in his ministry. But he didn't need them.

God needs men who are desperate for him and who are desolate without him. That's why, you see, there's a paradox throughout. Satan tried to get Jesus to do it the opposite way around, right at the beginning of his ministry. Satan said, "Now have a look round here. You can rule." And in terms of the world, he could have ruled. He could have had a quick empire which would have looked rather better than three years of work, ending up with 11 1/2 disciples who ran away. That was the temptation – to take control in the way men take control.

He resisted the temptation and said, "No, I'm going to do it God's way."

Why would we think there is a better way to rule the world than the one which God, in his wisdom, planned before time? It's through dying that men come to life. It's through the giving up of our lives. Mostly it is going to look foolish.

One of the things I encourage our people with is this: I say it is worth your whole life to minister to one old man the love of Jesus. If he swears at you for 20 years and you still go on loving him, that's worth your whole life, even if he doesn't come to Christ. Because that's what Jesus did for us. That's the heart that you minister in and of course, if you minister with a heart like that, the world will be won. He's chosen the weak because they don't have anything except Jesus.

"Jesus says, 'Will you give me your lunch?'"

Jackie Pullinger-To *on how God multiplies what we give*

The mystery of this particular ministry is that it multiplies grossly unfairly. It's like the loaves and the fishes. I often think about that little boy who was on the Mount with Jesus and those 5,000 men. I think about that little boy giving his fishes and his loaves. I think he thought he was giving his lunch to Jesus. He couldn't have known what was going to be done with it. We can see the figures and percentages of the starving in the world today and we feel threatened. We say, "I can't cope with that", and we do our little bit.

But Jesus says, "Will you give me your lunch?" That's all. The whole lunch. And when we share our whole lunch with him, 5,000 people are filled fit to bursting. That's how it works. It is the most illogical ministry I know. The multiplication is grossly out of proportion to the effort and heart that's put in because I think it has an ingredient of Jesus's heart. Personally, I think that the quickest way for world evangelism is through the poor. I'm absolutely convinced of it.

So where do you start? It is not a question of, "How do I help Ethiopia" or "Let's make a collection and send it to Jackie in Hong Kong." We don't want that. I'd be terribly disappointed if that was your response. I'm not saying we don't want your money but I don't want your collection instead of your broken heart for your neighbour. You just start with the one, and then there'll be another and another.

You know that the Lord has told us to heal the sick. We receive the power of the Spirit and we pray for the sick. When they're not healed, we go on praying for some more sick until we understand better spiritually how the Lord will work through us. We believe his promise anyway, whether the results we see are immediate or not. It is the same with ministering to the poor and feeding the hungry. You have to start somewhere. If we don't practise it, we won't get better at understanding how the Lord works it. One of the things I am absolutely certain that we as Christians are going to have to practise for the world to be saved, is multiplying food. I know you've practised casting out demons and healing the sick. Have you practised multiplying food?

Now, I am absolutely serious. Because if we wait until Christians have redistributed their wealth – our wealth – or the world has got a bit fairer in sending food wherever it's needed, still millions will have died. What would you say if you happened to be in a place where there are thousands of people and no food? You have to believe that the Lord has enough. You have to believe that it's perfectly all right to share what you've got by giving Jesus your lunch, and they'll be fed. But maybe he's not going to start you on those things right now.

Maybe he's going to start you on some little practices. That will be possible if we can get free from the fear of sharing what we've got, in case we don't have enough left.

Some years ago, a whole lot of Vietnamese refugees were put on an island in Hong Kong and this particular island had no water and no food. There were 6,000 and we heard from somebody that these people had no food and drink. As soon as I heard that those people were dying, I knew we had to do something. So I said to one of my colleagues, "Would you please ring up the government" – who were looking after the refugees – "and ask them how we can help." She came back and said, "The government were not very impressed by our phone call and said they don't want Christian do-gooders sending a little aid. They said that if you send oranges, you should send 6,000 or there will be a riot. And don't just send oranges once; you need to send them every day. Also, if you are going to send oranges, you must arrange your own transport." It is four hours by sea from Hong Kong.

So my colleague came back and said, "Shall we call a prayer meeting about this to see if we should do it?" I said, "No, we don't need a prayer meeting. They are our neighbours. We'll send 6,000 oranges daily from tomorrow onwards." You are supposed to help your neighbour. I then went and spoke to our accountant. He said, "If we send 6,000 oranges a day according to the money that we have, all of us will be starving within three days." All I can tell you is that we fed them for two months. I don't know how it happened. All I know is that money came in for the oranges; it came in and it went out so quickly. This is what it means when it says the right hand doesn't know what the left is doing. This is how it works.

Months later those refugees wrote to us. They knew what we'd done. We hadn't been allowed to preach the gospel, by the way. We didn't send little tracts with the oranges. We prayed over them, and those Vietnamese knew that they came from Jesus. How it worked, I can't tell you because actually we must be the poorest church in Hong Kong. But that's why we're the richest.

In the end, they moved the refugees to another place and they were OK. There was water and food. We didn't have to do it any more. The embarrassing thing was that we had, by this time, started an account called the 'Orange Account'. We ended up $100,000 over, so we gave it all to Ethiopia because we saw in the paper that there were people dying there. So you see how rich we are.

"Would you mind if I lay down on your bed and slept?"

Jackie Pullinger-To *on recognising our poverty*

I remember one time, there was one particular man, and I was really tired. I was actually exhausted. I said, "I'm really sorry, but I'm terribly tired. Would you mind if I lay down on your bed and slept?" So I lay down on his bed and slept. It was really nice because I was so tired. You know, after lying down on his bed I could do anything with those men because I was one of them. It was not a hard thing to do. It didn't matter that it was dirty cardboard and it smelled. It was his bed and he was awfully pleased to have something to offer me. It was very easy for him to receive prayer and rice because he could give me his bed. That is why I say that if we can recognise our own poverty, then we can minister with the poor.

"The Lord has answers to all this. Otherwise, I would have left years ago."

Chris Woods *on Christian leadership in an urban priority area*

Neither of my churchwardens had a telephone until a year ago. People don't have telephones where I live. To communicate in my parish, you have to go round and see them and if they are not there, you just have to go round again. It's very good for your figure. Now both church wardens have phones but one of their phones only takes incoming calls and you can't dial out on it. That's better than nothing. Those suffering the effects of poverty have no cars, no driving licences, no holidays, no credit, no telephones. One of our churchwardens, Eddie, has been out of work for 15 years. Before doing this job, I had never met Englishmen who didn't have a driving licence. If you have a driving licence, you can borrow a fellow Christian's car but if you haven't even got a licence, you're stuck and you are even more dependent upon somebody else. Some have no bank accounts and therefore no credit so they go to loan sharks for money. They borrow £100 and pay back £180 two months later. That's the nature of the loan shark game and it's very real. Broken limbs are the penalty for not paying up.

I had a woman come to my house with one of her six children. She was a widow whose husband had dropped dead walking out of the betting shop at the age of 43. She had come to Christ and while she was talking to me, her child ate her way through an entire packet of Penguin biscuits, one after the other. Meanwhile, her mother sat in my study, begging me for money to pay her rent. I said, "What's the problem?" and she told me that she gets her money from the social security on the Thursday and the rent man comes the next Tuesday. Of course, she should have put aside the money for the rent but she can't budget for five days ahead. She said she knew it was not a question of shortage of money. "It's just that I can't organise it," she said. Of course, we are all perfectly organised with our money, aren't we?

Then there is the effect upon the physical environment of living in an urban and industrial area. There is poor housing, heavy traffic, industrial pollution, factory chimneys, self-inflicted litter. Local authority decisions are taken by officials who do not live locally. When you are powerless, people take authority over you. This means that decisions are taken which vitally affect people – even about their houses and yet they have no power to overturn those decisions. There is widespread vandalism with wrecked playgrounds and excrement on swings. We had a car burned out in the yard behind the church. Our living room is right on the street and once two drunks fell off the pavement into the room through the window. When you hear running footsteps at 10 o'clock at night, you know something is wrong. On one occasion, a car had been picked up bodily and been tipped right over on its side. You may be feeling angry. It's the devil doing these things which makes us feel angry.

St Helens was identified in the *Daily Mirror* as the sickest town in Britain. There is widespread heavy smoking on top of the industry and traffic pollution. People live on a poor diet of junk foods. I've known a child who at midnight, ate five Mars Bars at one sitting. I've seen many children, including five year olds, with blackened stumps for teeth right to the gums. There are enormous numbers of grossly overweight people. It's desperate. Children start smoking at the age of nine. Other addictions like gambling (betting shops), glue sniffing and drugs are rife. We've been burgled over 20 times in the Vicarage. We've now got iron bars over the dining-room window which is where they get in. They need money to fund their addictions.

Then there are the video nasties. I had to go to a house where the six-year-old boy was suffering from what they called 'behavioural problems' at school. He was hitting people violently with rocks. I went to the house because I knew the mum vaguely – she is a single mum. This child was watching *Child's Play 3*, the video nasty which was linked to the James Bulger murder and to the murder of a 16-year-old girl in Manchester who was tortured for a week, then burned to death with petrol. In *Child's Play 3*, there is a demonic doll called Chucky and this child was watching the video right through, rewinding it back, watching it again and again. At the local school, he's called 'Chucky'. He has behavioural problems!

One of our sons had four bikes stolen in 16 months; then the garage where we kept them was burned down so that was the end of that. We now keep them in the house. There's a pub across the street called the Glass Barrel but the local name is the 'Blood Tub' because there have been three murders in there. I've buried a man who had his brains beaten out outside the 'Blood Tub'. There is a lot of domestic violence and many refuge centres for battered wives. I've buried three children run over in the street: a five-year-old who was run over playing on his own at 10.30 at night; a nine-year-old who was out even later was knocked over by a huge truck and another one during the day. These children run wild in the streets from the age of three upwards. They are completely unsupervised – and there's heavy traffic where we are. We had one 10-year-old who smashed 193 roof tiles on the brand new nursery school wing of the local primary school. He was the one who burned our garage down.

When we first arrived 17 years ago, my wife and I thought we must begin a youth club with snooker and so on. We'd already met one or two local families so we called about 10 or 12 together in an old disused school which we thought we might use as a venue. Within 40 minutes, they'd all fallen out with each other to such an extent that they got up and walked out except for me and one married couple. These were local parents trying to get together to organise a club for their children and they couldn't even have 40 minutes together without getting into such a state that they had to get up and walk out. It's coming from a lack of love and manifestation of love in their lives. Some of the people who have been Christians for ten years or so understand; they will tell you it is the presence of unforgiveness, unresolved hurts, bitterness, rejection, abuse from their childhood. If you tried to be a bit breezy with some of them, they wouldn't speak to you for six months. People are not secure so they can't take a joke at their own expense. I buried a man who had been married for 35 years but his wife, living in the same house as him, had not spoken to him for the previous 18 years before I took his funeral. Not a word. She had taken some vow, 'I'm not going to speak to you again' and didn't.

So we've had to work right through that. We've now seen people who have come to Christ becoming secure in the love of Jesus and the love of their fellow Christians. We have some wonderful times and there are some beautiful changes and healings in those areas. The Lord has answers to all this. Otherwise, I would have left years ago.

"At that stage, I used to say as we passed the plate around for the offering, 'If you haven't any money, take some out!'"

Chris Woods *on some of the principles, values and priorities important to his ministry in the UPA*

A ccepting people where they are. So many churches expect newcomers to behave like Christians as soon as they step across the door of the building. If they are smoking as they walk in, everyone throws up their hands in horror. But what do we expect? We must accept people as they are and then we will gradually seek to see change in various areas. Smoking comes about number 147 in our list of don'ts! One of our top ones is, 'Stop punching your wife.' That's a good one to start with after you've become a Christian!

We have 164 adults on our electoral roll, so it's not a big church. We grew fastest when we moved out of our church building (when the heating broke down) about ten years ago. We had to go into our church hall to worship. It was quite a convenient building and it didn't have that 'churchy' feel about it. They felt much more at home and they came in smoking, eating crisps and drinking Coke through the service. We didn't mind at all. At that stage, I used to say as we passed the plate around for the offering, "If you haven't any money, take some out!" and our giving kept on going up and up. It was amazing really. After I stopped saying that, the giving stopped going up as fast.

Discipling, Healing etc. We encourage people in the church to minister to one another and pray together to develop more maturity in Christ. Any number of one-to-one talks are going on at any given time during the week.

Intimate Relationship with God. It is important to value highly an intimate relationship with God through personal and corporate prayer and worship, walking in his ways and the fear of the Lord.

Experiencing God together. We seek to allow the Holy Spirit to move amongst us in restoration, healing and conviction of sin. John Wimber has helped us to see that the works of the devil are sin, sickness, demons and death, and the works of Jesus are forgiveness of sin, healing of the sick, driving out demons, raising the dead.

Freedom and Openness. We put no value in being legalistic or religious. We value flexibility and the desire to be open to God, to one another and to change. We also value integrity and accountability. One of the marks of brokenness in a Christian is flexibility and willingness to change. People who are totally inflexible are certainly not people who have been crucified with Christ, you'll find.

Servanthood. We have had to discourage those coming in from outside who have tried to run things rather than being prepared to serve. If you mix middle-class and working-class people, the former always dominate the situation. Many of the working class are so used to being told what to do, they sit on the church council and are quite happy to be dominated but I think that God is wanting to empower them to take decisions and be responsible. We have a very clear mutual accountability in recognising how we treat one another. We've had times of repenting of sin and attitudes.

Perseverance, Patience and Commitment. We value expressions of 'long-term faith', as in many areas of life and ministry, results are not quick.

Our first priority is **Worship and Prayer.** We spend more time, energy and money worshipping God than on any other activity. **Discipleship** is our second priority. There is no point in having fellowship together if people are going to fall out with each other. Discipleship comes before fellowship so that we can see some growth in Christian maturity. Then, when fellowship does take place, people are going to have a good time. **Fellowship** comes third.

Then there is **Outreach**: At a recent Alpha course we were electrified when 53 teenagers came in off the streets, straight into the church to see what was going on. We fed them tea and cream buns and we're taking them on! We're wrestling with the implications of how to lead this particular group but we praise God for them. It seems as if they've just come. They're local kids but they've never been near the church before except to throw stones at it.

Our other priorities are: pastoral care, training, counselling, inter-church unity, wider UK outreach and overseas mission. We believe that these priorities are helping us fulfil our purpose for being here, according to our stated values.

"I do not want South Africans ever to be able to say, 'We did it by our own right arms'...but rather that people would know it was the living God who intervened."

Michael Cassidy *on God's miracle in South Africa*

In the year King Uzziah died, I saw the Lord seated on a throne, high and exalted, and the train of his robe filled the temple. Above him were seraphs, each with six wings. With two wings they covered their faces, with two they covered their feet, and with two they were flying. And they were calling to one another: "Holy, holy, holy is the Lord Almighty: the whole earth is full of his glory." At the sound of their voices the doorposts and thresholds shook and the temple was filled with smoke. "Woe to me!" I cried. "I am ruined! For I am a man of unclean lips, and I live among a people of unclean lips, and my eyes have seen the King, the Lord Almighty." Then one of the seraphs flew to me with a live coal in his hand, which he had taken with tongs from the altar. With it he touched my mouth and said, "See, this has touched your lips; your guilt is taken away and your sin atoned for." Then I heard the voice of the Lord saying, "Whom shall I send? And who will go for us?" And I said, "Here am I. Send me!" (Isaiah 6: 1-8)

God gave us a mighty historical miracle during the South African elections. In 1994 we in South Africa lived through one of the most awesome and divine happenings in modern history; we moved overnight from the lip of the canyon of catastrophe into the most peaceful and crime-free five days in our history as our first democratic election took place, bathed in the miraculous love and reconciliation of the living God.

We do want to thank so many British Christians who stood by us, who prayed for us and expressed concern. There were many also who gave financial help. Maybe you would like to continue to pray as we are not out of the woods yet by a long way. There was an editorial in a major Sunday newspaper recently which said, "South Africa's transformation in one short year has been universally hailed as a miracle. It is hard to refute those who believe that events have been guided by a higher power who, still today seeks our harmonious co-operation towards a better future for all." That's from the *Sunday Tribune* in KwaZulu-Natal.

It is that divine involvement in the run-up to the April 1994 elections that I have sought to chronicle in my book (*A Witness For Ever*, Hodder and Stoughton) so that it might indeed stand as a witness for ever. The title is taken from Isaiah 38 where the

Lord speaks to the prophet and says, "Inscribe it on a tablet and write it in a book for the time to come as a witness for ever." I do not want South Africans ever to be able to say, "We did it by our own right arms. We have gotten ourselves this victory" but rather that people would know that it was the living God who intervened. If we start saying 'we' did it, it will be morally, socially and politically perilous.

The hard fact is that we need the Lord as much now or more than ever before. We have escalating and intensifying tensions and confusions that are building up once again, especially evidenced among young people in our country. And in KwaZulu-Natal the tensions between ANC and Inkatha Zulus could plunge us into a Rwanda-type scenario. Actually in the troubles in Rwanda in 1994, our team leader and his family were all lined up and shot. Other members of our team and Board were murdered. Some of our Board members were shot, our offices ransacked, our vehicles dsetroyed, computers taken, typewriters smashed. But our AE team there is again rising out of the ashes, praise God.

But now in South Africa itself the need we all have is for a fresh vision of God himself. We need to see who he is, to see what he does, to see how he does it, to see what he does and doesn't want us to do. We need to see what he expects from us, to discover where he would lead us, to discover what he wants us to say, to be and to do. There is always an interplay between the being and the doing. The doing has to come out from the being. Here especially do we need to grasp the truths of Isaiah 6, where the breakthrough vision of God came "in the year that King Uzziah died" (v 1) – in other words at a critical political moment when one dispensation was giving way to another. Always and everywhere, in times of change, bereavement or loss, marital trauma, financial pressure, social or political upheaval, emotional, psychological or spiritual crisis – when things we have held dear have died or are threatening to die, we need, like Isaiah, to see the Lord.

Our need is not to see Mandela or Clinton, or the House of Commons or the United States; our need is to see the Lord afresh. Our need beyond that is not to focus on Asuza Street or Toronto, Jonathan Edwards or history but on God. In South Africa, it is time for us to turn from our political miracle to the Lord behind the political miracle. Hosea 10:12 says, "It is time to seek the Lord." How then did Isaiah see this Lord? First of all, he saw him sitting on a throne high and lifted up. He lifted up his eyes to the throne and saw one who was a King, one who was Sovereign, one who was in charge and powerful and he had to bow down. It is a very important thing for us to grasp that God is Sovereign; he is in charge. I don't care what the problem is in your life today, God is in charge. He is not about to lose it in any way. He has his ways which are not human ways.

In our situation in South Africa God did something very unusual through a brother from Kenya named Washington Okumu. Few had really heard of Washington Okumu in South Africa. Everybody was looking to Henry Kissinger and Lord Carrington and other household names. Yet it was Washington Okumu, a Christian diplomat, through whom the breakthrough in human terms came in South Africa. It was Washington Okumu, a man of God around whom we had put a tremendous amount of prayer and who had taken time to invest in relationships and who had done things quietly behind the scenes, whom God used. I think that God looked out over South Africa and said, "Where is the weakest and frailest initiative and let's use that in some special way." It was precious how God just broke past all the big ones. We cannot rely just on politicians. We have to look to this living God. Isaiah saw him high and lifted up. He saw a God who was worthy of worship. Whenever I go into a church, I can monitor what's going on by the worship. We need a fresh spirit of worship throughout the world based on a new vision of who God is.

Isaiah saw the Lord as, "Holy, Holy, Holy". It's easy for us to trivialise the holiness of God or to trade on his mercy and forgiveness and to forget that the Holy Spirit is indeed the *Holy* Spirit. He wants to make us holy people. Jesus Christ is not just the baptiser in the Holy Spirit, he is the baptiser with fire. He seeks to burn away and scorch away the dross, impurity, hypocrisy, insincerity, laziness and lack of integrity which is rampantly in all of us. So it is absolutely, fundamentally and critically important that we see God afresh as one who rebukes our sinfulness, our idleness, our willingness to allow our society to go to hell while we just have a wonderful time as Christians. I believe it is so important that we take our faith right out into the societal arena and into the market place.

There were tremendous consequences for Isaiah once he had seen this Lord afresh. First of all, a deep conviction of sin and a need to confess came to him. He said, "Woe is me, I am lost." I believe we are all such lost people. That parable in Luke 15 [the lost sheep, the lost coin, the prodigal son] is not three parables, it is one. One parable in three parts on lostness: the sheep by nature, the coin by circumstances and the son by choice. Isaiah felt lost when he saw the holiness of God and he realised his sinfulness. He said, "I am a man of unclean lips." So often what is destroying us is what we say. It's our bitterness, our cynicism. Maybe it's not just a matter of how we use our lips but how we don't use our lips. We don't use our lips adequately in prayer or praise or testimony. Isaiah was aware that he dwelt in the midst of a people of unclean lips. If you don't think that you live in a people of unclean lips, turn your TV on any night. In South Africa, we are buying the whole garbage of what's coming in from the neo-pagan West. We need to repent of what we allow to be said from our own lips and from public forums in the land.

Then Isaiah, as he saw his lostness, called on God. We need to have a sense of, "Yes I too have sinned, failed, am lost." As soon as we come to that place, we are ready for a fresh experience of forgiveness. God can put away the past, or whatever is in the garbage department of your life or mine, by the precious blood of Jesus.

Then Isaiah had another wonderful consequence; he heard the voice of the Lord (v 8). We need to hear what is being said by God. There may be some of you who have been touched, blessed, had inner healing and all of that. But now you need to be ready to hear the voice of God afresh as he comes to us and he says, "Who will go for us and whom shall I send?" Many people are doing this, that and the next thing and there is no one to send.

But the Lord may be wanting to get our attention and have us hear his voice anew saying to us: "Go evangelise, seek the Spirit of God afresh, take a fresh stand for biblical morality and ethics, go prevent abortion on demand, go and speak to the government, go to the educationalists." "Who will go for us, whom shall I send?" was the divine cry heard by Isaiah. Most wonderfully he replied, "Lord here am I. Send me." When we come to this God and we get a fresh vision of him, we will surely hear his voice afresh and he will be saying, "Whom shall I send? Who will stand in the gap for me in this place?" Will you do it? Will you say today, "Lord here am I. Send me?"

And as you respond, don't forget also to speak prophetically to your nation, to kings, queens and prime ministers. It's not just enough for you to come to the Lord. Your nation must come to the Lord. If you don't bring your nation to the Lord then Britain is going to go down the tubes. South Africa is going to go down the tubes if we don't hold it for Jesus Christ at this time. Jesus said, "When the Holy Spirit comes upon you, you will be witnesses unto me in Jerusalem (where you are), in Judea (the area round about you), in Samaria (ie the people with whom you normally have no dealings) and to the uttermost parts of the world." That's the Holy Spirit's work. As the Holy Spirit comes upon us and is released within us, so then rivers of living water will flow out from our innermost beings to touch people around us. That's what he wants and as we go out we will be saying several things in our testimony.

What sort of things are we going to say? I believe that in this neo-pagan, effectively atheistic age, the first thing we have to do is to say that *God is there*, is alive, is real because we are in an environment that is atheistic. The Bible says, "The fool has said in his heart, there is no God." Atheists can't be consistent with their presuppositions. I heard about a man thundering from his soap box in Hyde Park Corner and he said, "My great-grandfather was an atheist and so was my grandfather. So was my father and thank God, I'm an atheist too." Well, we for our part have to say that God is really there! We have to be a witness to a God who is. Then, we have to say that *God is powerful.* He is in charge and he can do incredible things. He is powerful to change us in our hearts through the new birth as he blesses us, sanctifies us, gives us inner healing, fresh experiences of the Holy Spirit and blessings in the supernatural. God has power. Jesus said, "I have all power on heaven and on earth." There is no problem we can bring that our Lord Jesus cannot deal with.

This God to whom we come is also moral and holy. The ten commandments are not the ten suggestions. We need to make that very clear to our society and seek constantly to re-embrace it ourselves. God's laws are written not only in the Bible but in the fabric of the universe. Then I believe we have to say that this God is the God and Father of our Lord Jesus Christ. 1 Peter 1:3 says, "Blessed be the God and Father of our Lord Jesus Christ." See what Jesus is like and you know what God is like. He is all power in heaven and on earth. "Without him was not anything made that was made." I remember when I saw Niagara Falls that it was a religious experience. When I saw that, I worshipped. When I saw Victoria Falls I said, "Jesus you are marvellous." When I snorkled in the Great Barrier Reef, I tried to praise God mightily underwater and nearly drowned! Before you die, you have got to try and see the Great Barrier Reef and you will never believe what God has put under the sea – the marvels of those coral reefs. Jesus is the creator of all that. Praise his name. He is all powerful. Our creator Lord.

Last year, when we called the huge pre-election prayer meeting in South Africa, people wanted to call it the 'Interfaith Rally'. But we said, "No, it's got to be the *Jesus Peace Rally*." Then some tried to make it an 'Interchurch Rally' but we said there's no power in the word 'interchurch'. The power is in the name of Jesus. Indeed, there is no other name given among men whereby we may be saved. As we come to the cross of Jesus, there is forgiveness no matter what anyone has done. I don't care what you have done. The blood of Jesus cleanses from all sin. Then there is the resurrection to tell us that he is alive. And Pentecost tells us that the Holy Spirit is available to fill, flood and transform, and take us all to a new place. Let this be the year and the moment we all see the Lord afresh. The consequences could be awesome not only in our personal lives, but in our churches and in our nations.

"If God called you into finance and you become a preacher, that isn't the highest calling in the world. It's actually to reject the highest calling."

Steve Chalke *on working in the world*

The essential quality of a leader that marks him or her apart from those they lead is simply this: they know where they are going; they are able to see the future; they have that gift of foresight and direction. A leader by virtue of the name *has* to be going somewhere. What we have been called to do corporately is to lead society. We are 'Jesus' for the UK and for the world.

Everybody has got dreams of where they want to be headed, but a leader isn't someone who just has an idea about what is going to happen in the future – a leader is someone who knows *how* to deal with the future. Without leadership we become victims of what's happening; with leadership we become architects of our own future.

We slowly tend to get out of touch with what is really happening out there. Every time I get in my car, if I listen to a worship or a ministry tape and that is my whole diet, I slowly become isolated from the culture that I am called to reach and understand. Listen to your tapes but also to your radio. Listen to what is going on in the world around you. Be good judges of the times – that is what leadership is all about. Winston Churchill said, "Always listen to your best friends and your worst enemies because they are both telling you the truth about yourself from a slightly different perspective."

We need happy hearts but we need heads that are wise and full. The following passage is called 'The Jesus Manifesto'. Jesus wants to sum up all he is going to be doing in the next three years. This is what he is about: "The Spirit of the Lord is upon me because he has anointed me to preach the Good News to the poor. He has sent me to proclaim freedom to the prisoners. The recovery of sight to the blind. To release the oppressed. To proclaim the year of the Lord's favour for people." (Luke 4:18-19)

If this was Jesus's manifesto, his job description, how he summed up what he was going to spend his life doing, then we've got to take it in and think about it hard. Why? Because now we are Jesus for the world. We are the body of Christ. Jesus's manifesto must be our manifesto. Otherwise we're about something other than what Jesus was about.

All service is Christian service. At Oasis we run a training course for Christian youth ministers. It's a two year course, accredited by a university. Someone came to do the course from a church I know. His cousin at the same time went and did a youth and community degree, basically the same course as we run, but he went to do it with Suffolk College where it is a purely secular course. Throughout the last two years, the entire church has been praying for the guy that's been in our Christian youth and community course. At no point, has anyone even acknowledged that the other guy is on a course. Why? Because we've divided the world neatly into Christian and non-Christian bits.

So we say, "This is to do with 'spiritual' things. It's not about terrible things like housing or homelessness. It's not about issues of economic problems or fair trading." But Jesus comes along and says, "You've got it all wrong because you've tried to divide up my world just like your culture tells you to."

But it isn't that way. These verses are true spiritually and they are also true politically. They are true socially and economically. They are true materially and emotionally. These verses are true at every level and the task of the church, if it is to be like Jesus, is, "That you are anointed by God's Spirit so that you can bring good news to the poor." That's what it means at every level so that you can proclaim freedom, proclaim recovery of sight to the blind.

Biblically, the truth is this: if I am called to preach, I'd better preach and that is the highest calling in the world as far as I am concerned because God called me to be it. But, if God called you to be an engineer, if God called you to be a pilot, a nurse, a doctor, a plumber, a builder, or to work in advertising, in graphics, in law, business, industry; if God called you into finance and you become a preacher, that isn't the highest calling in the world. It's actually to reject the highest calling.

All we get is a little bit more withdrawn from the world, all we get is a little less salt in society and one more useless preacher who is going to bore people stupid for the next 50 years when he or she should be out there in the world.

If God called you to be in the police force, stay in the police force and strive for excellence there because we need people who will understand that God has got something to say about law and order, justice and righteousness. If God called you to be in the world of finance, don't just say, "I'm doing my bit but actually I help out at the Sunday school at HTB. That's where I *really* serve God." Get in that bank, stay in that bank, strive for excellence in what you do and apply Jesus's ethics. Apply all that the Bible has to say to that world in which you work.

You may ask, "Well how do I do it? It's really hard." I know it's really hard. If it was easy we would have cracked it before. I am not a banker, I know nothing about banking; I can't even keep my own bank account in order. But there are some of you in this room who are good at banking. What the Bible is telling you is that you are to be Jesus in that world of finance because we are to be light and salt. We are to bring truth at every level. We are to set free those who are financially oppressed. We are to drive back unrighteousness in every level. Then it will transform what you do from Monday and Friday into something you must strive for excellence in.

What about all the people who are out there, working? Are they serving God or not? Of course they're serving God and they are on the cutting edge. Prayer meetings tend to be to pray for the pastors: "Let's pray for the full time workers of the church, they're on the cutting edge." Everyone prays for them and that is great. Then you pray for the missionaries serving in Africa and places like that. So you pray for the church leaders and you pray for the missionaries. Nobody even knows where everybody else works, let alone prays for them!

We, as pastors, ministers, curates, are *not* on the front line. If you read Ephesians 4:11-12, you discover there that Paul says we are on the back line: "Some evangelists, some prophets, some pastors, some teachers ... all of these people are there to equip the church for the work of ministry." They are there in a back-up role. They are there to equip the church for its service on the front line. Where is the front line? It's in the local school, hospital, bank, – that's where the church is working, where the front line is. The problem is that the whole church has been looking the wrong way for too long. We are utterly confused. We think the back line is the front line and we think the front line hardly exists at all.

Our church leaders have made two errors. Our first is in our assessment of the situation. We have over-estimated the role we play and under-estimated the role that everybody else is supposed to play. The next error is the error of empowerment. Because when you don't notice that the front line actually is the front line, you don't bother to empower the people. You don't pray for them, you don't equip them. So there's a lady sitting in the church, she's got enormous issues at work, hiring and firing people. Nobody even knows what she does. They don't acknowledge this is the front line.

We need TV presenters but the presenter is at the end of a very long chain; we need Christian producers, we need directors, editors, researchers, programme controllers, people in PR, people running agencies. That's where we have to invest our strength. When someone gets into the world of media or the world of arts, it's not, "Oh well, there goes another one…" it means there is another one on the front line. When someone gets involved in the world of finance, education, nursing, medicine, there's another person on the front line.

A boy called John at 14 years of age, heard a sermon on mission work. He said, "God, I don't really want to be a missionary, I want to be a builder. Even though no one has mentioned that building is of any importance to you, and it seems utterly unimportant, I'd really like to be a good builder. If I make it, I promise you Lord that I'll invest everything I've got for you."

His name was John Laing. Laings became the biggest building company in the world. London Bible College was built on John Laing's money. Colleges and churches all over Great Britain and around the world were built because one 14-year-old boy knew that he wasn't a write-off because he didn't want to be a preacher.

The poem, 'The Gas Lamp Lighter' by Robert Louis Stevenson, gives a mental image of this gas lamp lighter wandering the streets, slowly punching hole after hole in the darkness until the whole place is ablaze with light. That's what we're about. That's what Jesus is talking about. You are called to punch holes in the darkness. You are called to serve him, called to give your best to your King.

Jesus said, "The spirit of the Lord is on me and he has anointed me to preach good news, to set free the oppressed, to proclaim liberty to the captives, to announce that this is the year of the Lord's favour." Spiritually, materially, physically, emotionally, economically, politically, we are to bring the good news, to bring justice. That's what we're about. We are all on the front line.

The power of the Spirit

"Paul ... would not have understood a Christian faith in which the experienced life of the Spirit was not the key to every dimension of that life."

Gordon Fee *on the Holy Spirit in Paul's epistles*

I was born and raised in a Pentecostal preacher's home. He was a unique pastor in the American Assemblies of God in that he read good books and preached out of the good, hard work that he did on the biblical text. I look back on that and recognise that I had the unique experience of being exposed to good biblical teaching in the context of which the power and the presence of God was welcomed, sought and desired.

Even so, the idea of being an academic was about as far removed from my personal history as one could get. The Pentecostals saw the dangers of young men and women on fire for God going away and getting their heads screwed up somewhere and losing that passion. I knew that, whatever else, I didn't want to lose that passion. On the other hand, when Jesus said, "Love the Lord your God with all your heart and with all your mind." I always felt it was a bit of a shame that we Pentecostals loved God with all our hearts, but cut off our heads and threw them away, as it were.

One day, when I was in my fourth year of pastoring a church, I walked into my church study – it was right after lunch – and picked up the mail. Amongst it was a copy of *Christianity Today* and I was sort of glancing through it when I came across the name of a fellow minister of my own denomination who had written a letter. It was one of these typical Pentecostal letters, excoriating *Christianity Today* for its egg-head Christianity. He concluded his letter with these words: "I would rather be a fool on fire than a scholar on ice!"

In that moment the Holy Spirit spoke into my heart and I dropped my head on my desk and I wept and wept. The Holy Spirit said, "There are two other options." I had seen fools on ice, but I had never seen a scholar on fire. In a deep calling and commitment I said, "Lord, if that is possible, I would be one of those."

So the pilgrimage has been a long one. I received my PhD from an American university in 1966 in New Testament Studies and became the first person from the Pentecostal tradition who had received a university PhD in Biblical Studies.

About eight years ago, in response to an invitation by a group of friends, I sat down to write an article on the Pauline texts with a particular emphasis on the Spirit in those letters. And I discovered two things.

First of all, I discovered that there was no book on this subject anywhere. It didn't exist. That surprised me to no end because you would think that everything in New Testament scholarship had been done by the year 1988. What new rock would you look under for something new? But there was no book on the Holy Spirit and Paul. There were books on Pauline theology that had very small sections on the Spirit. There were books on the Spirit in the New Testament that had their appropriate Pauline sections, but there were no books on the Spirit in Paul. Later I was invited by a publisher to beef up that article. I had no idea this book was going to go as long as it did. I figured a 500 page book. I had no idea a 900 page book was coming out of this.[1] The working on that material changed my life.

The idea that you can talk about Paul and not talk about the experience of the Spirit is a scholarly absurdity. What makes

[1] *God's Empowering Presence*, Paternoster Press

Paul tick is the experience of the Spirit. If that doesn't objectify very well, that is our problem. You can't read Paul very long without recognising that it is the experience of the Spirit that lies right at the heart of things.

That doesn't mean the very heart. Paul does not say, "For me to live is the Spirit." He says, "For me to live is Christ."

But the Spirit has been marginalised both in New Testament scholarship and in Christian theology – particularly when it comes to Paul's theology.

In traditional Christian theology (particularly from the Reformation), we pay perfectly decent lip-service to the Spirit. But we keep the Spirit at a safe distance in our creeds and theology to keep him out of the life of the church.

We want to be in control of the life of the church and the Spirit won't always let us do that. That makes us nervous!

So what developed in the church is the quietest view of the Spirit. To use the imagery of Moses from Exodus: that God was not in the wind, the fire, the earthquake – but in the still small voice.

Now what absolutely intrigues me is that that passage from the Old Testament has become the major theological centre for understanding the Spirit in most Protestant theologies.

That *Old Testament* passage, mind you. And nobody even blinks doing that kind of hermeneutics, but we are comfortable with the still, small voice. And in doing so, we have marginalised the Spirit in our understanding of Paul. We just haven't been fair to the apostle.

We have run out of steam by being primarily Binitarian and not Trinitarian. We believe in the Father and the Son, and believe in the Holy Spirit, but do not recognise the central role the Spirit plays in Pauline theology.

I came to the conclusion (and I might be quite wrong) that the key to this generally quiescent attitude towards the Spirit lies in a failure to take seriously the Spirit as person and presence.

The Spirit, after all, is a word to which we don't relate very well. We think of the first two persons of the Trinity who, because of the incarnation we know and image in relational terms as father and son. There is a kind of general fuzziness in the church with regards to the Spirit.

Many years ago when I was first teaching in a denomination school, a Pentecostal student came to one of my colleagues and said, "God the Father I understand. God the Son I can relate to. But the Holy Spirit is a grey oblong blur."

For Paul, the Spirit was none other than God's personal presence. He never thought impersonally of the Spirit. We do, but he didn't.

Some say, "We believe that the real reason for the Spirit is to produce the fruit of the Spirit" and the others are saying, "We need to have the gifts of the Spirit." But we need both. What kind of reading of Paul can you imagine would ever bring about that 'either/or'? Paul wouldn't understand us.

For Paul, the Spirit was an experienced empowering reality. Paul would not have understood most historic Protestantism. I know that is unkind but it is true.

The reason he wouldn't have understood it is because he would not have understood a Christian faith in which the experienced life of the Spirit was not the key to every dimension of that life.

Look at the way Paul argues in Galatians chapter three. He begins with the experienced life of the Spirit. He says in verse two, "This alone I want to learn from you. Did you receive the Spirit by works of the law or by the hearing of faith?"

Do you understand that when he says, "Did you receive the Spirit?" that's where most of us would say, "Did you get saved?" "Did you become a believer?" That is his way of talking about becoming a believer. He doesn't understand Christian faith that doesn't think first in terms of "Did you receive the Spirit?"

This was a visible and experienced reality. It is certain by the way the rest of the argument unfolds. "Having begun in the Spirit are you going to come to completion by the flesh?" (which in this case is a play on circumcision).

Our English translations tend to fail us here. Verse four – Paul does *not* say, "Did you suffer so much in vain?" [as it is translated in the NIV]. There is no evidence of suffering anywhere in Galatians. This is the Greek word for experience. He says, "Have you experienced so many things in vain?" Then, typically, he says, "If indeed it is in vain" – and he knows it isn't.

Now listen to what he has done. He has appealed to the beginning point of their conversion. "Did you receive the Spirit?" Then he says, having begun that way, "Do you become now completed by works of law?"

So he goes back and reminds them of their conversion in-between. "Have you experienced so much in vain?"

Then verse five turns all of this into the present tense. Therefore, based on the appeal to experience in verse four, Paul says, "He who supplies you with the Spirit and works miracles among you, does he do this by adherence to works of law or by the hearing of faith?"

This was so presuppositional for Paul, he doesn't even bat an eye. He simply begins by aiming straight at their experienced life.

Now that is the passage that reminds me of how far we are from them in understanding New Testament Christianity. I am not a Pentecostal who is talking about, "You have got to get baptised in the Spirit or you are not with it."

I am talking about what is absolutely essential, at the heart of Christian faith. That is the experienced empowering reality of the Spirit of the Living God. That is not some addendum, some extra.

"Nothing else can take the place of presence."

Gordon Fee *on the presence of God*

I would like to look at the understanding of the presence of God as a motif in the Old Testament. That begins in Genesis when, because of human fall, the presence is removed. God doesn't walk with them any more.

Presence is a delicious word because it points to one of our truly great gifts. Nothing else can take the place of presence – not gifts, not telephone calls, not pictures, not reminding mementoes, nothing.

Ask the person who has lost a lifelong mate what they have missed the most. The answer invariably is presence.

When we are ill, we don't need soothing words nearly as much as we need loved ones to be present. What makes shared life, games, walks, concerts, outings and the myriad of other things, so pleasurable? Presence. God has made us this way. What we lost in the garden was the most significant expression of presence of all and that is the presence of God.

Can you understand that when you read the Psalmists they do not cry out to go to the Temple and sacrifice? They cry out to go to the Temple because God is there. "My soul longs for the Living God."

They long to come and appear before God. "Oh, a day in your courts is better than a thousand elsewhere." They long to be in the presence of the Living God.

Friends, this is what makes the fall of Jerusalem and the exile such a tragedy. Because with the fall of Jerusalem and the destruction of the Temple, the Jewish people lost the place of the presence.

They were no longer identifiable as a people of the presence. They did become a people of the Book – we can thank God for that. But they were not a people of the presence. They thrust this longing for the presence right out into the future.

The key passage, the one that I want you to note now, is Isaiah 63. Because at the end of the prophesies of Isaiah, we have this incredible thing that has taken place in Old Testament understanding, namely that the presence of God in the Tabernacle and the Temple is none other than the Spirit of God himself.

I pick this oracle up in Isaiah 63:9: "He became their Saviour in all their distress. It was no angel or messenger but his presence that saved them. In his love and mercy he redeemed them. He lifted them up and carried them all the days of old. Yet they rebelled and grieved his Holy Spirit."

That is the language Paul picks up in Ephesians 4:30 "Do not grieve the Holy Spirit of God." That comes right out of that text. They grieved the Holy Spirit.

Then you go down to Isaiah 63:11 and he says, "Where is he who brought them through the sea (This is speaking now of the presence) with the shepherd of his flock (which is Moses)? Where is he who set his Holy Spirit among them?" (That is referring to the presence) Finally in v 14: "Like cattle that go down to the plain, the Spirit of Jahweh gave them rest." (Referring to their entering into the land).

The fulfilment of these Spirit expectations are crucial to Paul's understanding of what it means to be the people of God in the new covenant.

"We get to cooperate with God in what he is trying to do..."

Sandy Millar *on working with God in the ministry of the Holy Spirit*

> Then he took them [the disciples] with him and they withdrew by themselves to a town called Bethsaida, but the crowds learned about it and followed him. He welcomed them and spoke to them about the kingdom of God and healed those who needed healing. Late in the afternoon the Twelve came to him and said, "Send the crowd away so they can go to the surrounding villages and countryside and find food and lodging, because we are in a remote place here!" He replied, "You give them something to eat!" They said, "We have only five loaves and two fish." But he said to his disciples, "Make them sit down in groups of about 50 each." The disciples did so and everyone sat down. Taking the five loaves and two fish and looking up to heaven he gave thanks and broke them. Then he gave them to his disciples to set before the people. They all ate and were satisfied and the disciples picked up twelve baskets full of broken pieces that were left over. (Luke 9:10-17)

This story, amongst many others of course, is a basis for the ministry of the Spirit. It was a foretaste, in a sense, of what Jesus was doing and was going to do, and still does. It is fascinating to consider the agonies the disciples must have gone through. I don't know at what point it dawned on them that there was a link between the 5,000 men – plus women and children – and these five loaves and two little fish. I don't know whether they all came to the same conclusion at the same minute but somewhere along the line, it must have occurred to them, "He's going to ask us to feed them with these five loaves and two fish!" Which is sure enough what he did.

The point I want to make is that at every stage, two things were operating. One was that Jesus – graciously, wonderfully, kindly – was inviting them to cooperate with him if they wanted to. Secondly, he was helping them to see that without him they would fall flat on their faces. You know, I know and everybody knows that you can't feed 5,000 men with five loaves and two fish. What I love to imagine is the moment at which that truth dawned on them.

When we talk about a ministry of the Spirit, we're talking about cooperation with God. Jesus was saying to them, "We have a wonderful opportunity here. Cheer up, smile, we've got 5,000 hungry people, and we've got five loaves and two fish. Why don't we feed them?" They said to him, "You feed them." They each thought it was up to the other to feed them. Jesus was saying, "Why don't we both feed them. We'll do it together." So it's cooperation coupled with an understanding that without him we can do nothing. That's why we are so constantly vulnerable. But it's also why the only thing worth holding out for is the ministry of the Spirit.

On a trip to Poland some time ago, I met a dear lady. I should think she was about 75, dressed in black and with a wrinkled brown face. We were in a conference hall of about 3,500 people. We were praying for anybody who appeared and people kept appearing and asking to be prayed for. It was at one level a frustrating thing and, at another level, an opportunity to rediscover the sort of feeling of the feeding of the 5,000. All we had to do was to pray for them. I can only say that I haven't seen God work in that way for a very long time, if ever. They kept coming and we prayed for them and God did something. Now I didn't do anything except pray for them but I think that was my function because cooperation is the essence of the ministry of the Spirit.

This lady came up and the interpreter said, "She wants you to pray for her left eye," which was twitching. We hadn't much time because there were a lot of people; I looked at her left eye and I asked the Spirit of God to come and do whatever he wanted to do for her. Into my head came the next question, "How long have you had that?" She replied, "About two years." I said, "Did something happen two years ago?" and she said, "My husband died."

So as I prayed the Spirit down on her, it became perfectly clear to me that her twitching left eye was a symptom of a broken heart. Into my head came God's promise, "I will bind up the broken hearted." That is his ministry and we get the privilege of sharing with that ministry. I said, "Lord, would you bind up her broken heart." I can only tell you if you'd seen that woman as I left her, you would have seen that she was with the Lord. There was nothing I had done. I left her in seventh heaven! She was together with God which is what God wanted. He's jealous for her. She's his. She's of formal Roman Catholic background and he loves her and was working in her heart, doing something in her and for her. Her eye stopped twitching when her heart was healed. It was a great blessing to me just to watch and to be able to leave her safely in the hands of the Lord and move onto somebody else.

It was like that in the feeding of the 5,000, if I can put it humbly in that way. We get to cooperate with God in what he is trying to do. It's all the way through the Bible. You remember Moses? Moses was continuously being called to cooperate with God. You remember when he got to the river? God said to him, "Moses, hold out your stick over the water." Why? Doesn't it sound stupid? Why should Moses hold his stick out over the water? I don't know. If I'd been Moses, I'd have said, "Well Lord, why don't you just part the water and get on with it because the Egyptians are coming, and I've got better things to do than stand here." By which he would mean of course, "I don't want to look foolish. There's a big river here and I've got a stick, and I'm just standing. I know that you told me to do this but they don't know you told me, they think I'm just doing it, trying to pretend that this is what you do!"

But somehow there was a dynamic going on that if he did that, God would do the rest. You see it again and again with the saints, the Old Testament prophets, the disciples. They got to cooperate and still get to cooperate with what God is trying to do. At the end of the day, Paul seems to suggest, that is the basis of Christian ministry. The kingdom doesn't consist of words. Paul says it's about power. It isn't that we're power hungry. We believe that God wants to change people and it's immensely frustrating to go on talking and for nothing to change. It's still pretty frustrating from time to time, but that is the basis and the essence of the thing.

I had been ordained for two years when a man who lived nearby, rang up and asked if he could come and see me. I said, "Yes, of course." He said, "I need advice badly. I've just lost my job. My wife has just told me that she can't bear it any longer and I've got two children at schools which I don't know that I'll be able to pay for. I'm very worried." I thought to myself, "And you want to come and see me?" I said, "Lord, you've got about about five minutes because he's coming from number 67." I had nothing to set before him. That is the context for every understanding and receiving of spiritual gifts. I have nothing to set before them. This woman has a twitching left eye. Well, I can't heal twitching left eyes! It is a matter of cooperating with the Lord.

"Do we really believe that what we read in the Bible is true and actually works?"

J. John *on the Word and the Spirit*

Did you know that when Charles Darrow brought the first prototype of the board game Monopoly to Parker Brothers in 1934 they laughed him out of their offices? They said, "That is really a stupid game! It is never going to sell. It is far too complicated. It takes far too long to play. We are experts on games and we have found 52 major flaws in this game."

But Charles Darrow said, "Well, it doesn't matter what you say, because I believe in it. I will market the game by myself." Within one year, one department store sold 5,000 sets. It was such a hit that Parker Brothers confessed, "Well, maybe we were a little too hasty." So they signed a contract with Charles Darrow – who became a multi-millionaire – and they have since sold over 100 million sets of Monopoly in 54 countries and in 26 languages.

What have you got faith in? What have you got confidence in? Do we have confidence in Jesus Christ? Do we actually have confidence in the Word of God? Do we actually have confidence in his Holy Spirit? Do we really believe that what we read in the Bible is true and actually works? Charles Darrow had confidence in a game. Even though he was turned down, it didn't matter. He had confidence and he persevered and he saw all that fruit.

I have been reading recently how we got the Bible. It was so good to be reminded of people like John Wycliffe, the Oxford theologian and 14th-century English religious reformer, who first translated the entire Bible into English in 1382. Wycliffe was not acclaimed by his contemporaries. Three decades after his death, Wycliffe's bones were dragged from their grave and were burned. What had been Wycliffe's crime? He had dared to translate the Bible into a language people could understand. It had been Wycliffe's passionate desire that everyone should be free to read the good news of eternal life through faith in Christ. His hand-copied Bible was circulated widely and eagerly read – all before the days of printing.

William Tyndale began the printing of the New Testament in 1525. It was the first English translation ever to be made directly from the original Greek. Copies of Tyndale's testament were smuggled into England in barrels. They were widely distributed and eagerly studied. But then church leaders ordered that they should all be burned. In May 1535 Tyndale was imprisoned. He was tried for heresy and condemned to death. A decade earlier they had burned the translation. Now they resolved to burn the translator. Tyndale went boldly to the stake still defending his belief that people should have a Bible in their own language. On 6 October 1536 he was tied to a post and strangled, after which his body was burned.

Through the centuries courageous men and women have treasured the scriptures and have struggled to preserve and distribute them amidst great opposition. The Bible is a precious heritage and a priceless gift. The once forbidden book now lies open to each of us to feed from. Isn't that remarkable?

In Psalm 119, verse 105, it says, "Your Word is a lamp to guide me and a light for my path." Many people find the Bible very difficult. But I have been a Christian for 22 years and I have worked something out: if the Bible says 'no', it means no. If the Bible says 'yes', it means yes. If it doesn't say 'yes' or 'no', God doesn't mind. If our Bible is falling apart then we won't be.

In the Bible, it says seven times, "This is the Will of God." One of those occasions is in Ephesians 5:17-18 when it says,

"...Understand what the Lord's will is: do not get drunk on wine; instead be filled with the Holy Spirit." What does it mean to 'get drunk'? It means that you are under the control and influence of alcohol.

What does it mean to 'be filled with the Spirit'? You are under the influence and control of God. Have you noticed that when someone is drunk they have a lot of courage? When you are filled with the Holy Spirit you have a lot of courage. Have you noticed that drunk people love to sing? When you are filled with the Holy Spirit you love to sing.

I went to India a couple of years ago. I had a terrible time. I came back with dysentery. I was so ill that when Killy [his wife] picked me up at the airport I could hardly push the trolley. I vowed that I wouldn't go back to India.

When the Kansas City prophets came to HTB [a conference on prophecy in 1991] I was at the conference. After the first day, I thought, "I really want to meet with God. I am going to get up early and seek you Lord before I go to the conference." The next morning, I got up. I had my Bible. I thought, "Oh Lord, it is so early in the morning and I don't know what to read." So I closed my eyes and opened it at random – something I usually tell people not to do! I opened my eyes and read Isaiah 54:2-3: "Enlarge the place of your tent, stretch your tent curtains wide, do not hold back; lengthen your cords, strengthen your stakes. For you will spread out to the right and to the left."

When I got to the HTB conference, I was asked, "Would you like to meet these prophets?" I said, "Yes." There were about five of them. I sat there. One of them got up and said, "I have got a word from God for you: Isaiah 54:2-3. 'Enlarge the place of your tent, stretch your tent curtains wide, do not hold back; lengthen your cords, strengthen your stakes. For you will spread out to the right and to the left.' Does that mean anything to you?" Hmmmm. Then the next one got up and said, "You are going to go to India. When you go to India it is going to change your life." I said, "He's not a prophet because, if he was, he would know I do not want to go to India."

That was five years ago. I went to India this year. It has radically changed my life. The first conference I went to had 15,000 people. Eight thousand were seriously sick. I went to another conference and there were 200,000 at this conference. The word multitude has taken on a whole new meaning. The sick were healed en masse. The paralytic got up and walked. The eyes of the blind were opened. There was worship, preaching and signs and wonders accompanied the preaching of the Word.

This is the God of the Bible. We can root all of this into the Bible. The Bible brings Jesus to us and makes him alive and real. What Jesus did then, the Holy Spirit continues to do now. He wants to stretch out his hand today and nourish us and inspire us and do things deep within our hearts. And touch us spiritually, emotionally and psychologically and physically.

Recently my son Simeon broke his leg and had it in plaster. We went for a check up with the doctor two weeks after he had the plaster on to see how it was doing. The doctor took two X-rays and said, "I am sorry, but we are going to have to take the cast off and re-set it because the leg has moved. We are going to have to do it today, otherwise the leg will set and we will have to break it." He said, "I just need to pop out, but I will be back in five minutes."

I said, "Simeon, we've got five minutes." We laid hands on his legs and this was no 'messing about' prayer. It was "Lord Jesus, fix this leg. Lord, sort his leg out now." Then the doctor walked in and said, "Let me just take one more X-ray." He took another X-ray, put it up on the screen and said, "W... Well, ... We don't have to take the cast off after all." I said, "While you were out I consulted another physician." He asked, "Who was that?" I said, "In the Bible he is known as the Great Physician." What an encouragement to Simeon and to me. That is our Jesus.

The great church elder, Tertullian, said in the third century AD: "The two hands of God the Father are the Word and the Spirit". The Word tells us that our Jesus did all this and the Spirit continues to do it today – in different ways. The will of God is that we be filled – intoxicated – with his Holy Spirit and that we be released to love and serve him in the world through word and deed.

"I don't think I've been to any real living, believing church where there were not prophetic people in the midst, placed there by the Lord Jesus."

Steve Nicholson *on prophecy*

Therefore, my brothers be eager to prophesy – 1 Corinthians 14:39

To me, prophetic ministry is nothing more than one more tool in the tool box of bringing God's kingdom and God's mercy to people. It's not the most important thing necessarily. It's not the thing we should focus on. In fact, its prime function is really to point us towards Jesus and to give us a greater revelation of who he is.

It was he [Jesus] who gave some to be apostles, some to be prophets, some to be evangelists, and some to be pastors and teachers, to prepare God's people for works of service, so that the body of Christ may be built up until we all reach unity in the faith

and in the knowledge of the Son of God and become mature,
attaining to the whole measure of the fulness of Christ. (Ephesians
4:11)

Jesus gives these gifts – and wherever there is a living,
believing church, he does not cheat or short change us. I don't
think I've been to any real living, believing church where there
were not prophetic people in the midst, placed there by the
Lord Jesus because he loves his church. He loves us. He cares
about us. He wants to help us. He never intended that our lives
should be bereft of that sense of the presence of God, and his
working and acting among us.

The point of all this is of course, so that the body of Christ
will be built up. He wants us to be stronger. He wants us to be
more encouraged, to be more full of faith, to be healed. Even
more important, it is to help us grow up in the knowledge of the
Son of God. It's to help reveal Jesus himself – who he really is.

Paul says: In the church, "pursue love and desire spiritual
gifts, especially that you may prophesy." (1 Corinthians 14:1)
"Especially that you may prophesy?" Why? Because it is so
beneficial. And in 1 Corinthians 14:3, he says, "But everyone
who prophesies speaks to men for their strengthening,
encouragement and comfort." It's important to keep in mind
here in the New Testament, that the function of the prophetic
gift is not entirely the same as the function in the Old Testament. New Testament prophets are not necessarily bringing
judgement on the nations. Their main function is to do these
three things: (i) to bring a strengthening, encouragement and
comfort to the body of Christ; (ii) to build us up, to make us
stronger in faith; (iii) to draw us closer to Jesus, to bring
comfort and healing and restoration to us.

I've known something of prophecy all my life but it was
fairly intermittent and not very strong. I'd heard stories about
some of those folks down in Kansas City [where a strong
prophetic ministry had grown] and my first reaction was like a

lot of people, "Well, I'm never going to have anything to do with that!" So one day, God spoke to me and said, "Why are you judging people you have never even met?" So I started repenting of my judgements on people and then I began to find that somewhere inside, I was really frustrated being a leader of a church and always feeling like I was stumbling around in the dark in terms of what was really going, what was happening spiritually. Everything was always catching me like I was a blind man. I said, "Lord, you know, what is this?" and he said, "Well, you know you're blind. You don't have the bodily equivalent of eyes which is the prophetic ministry." So I started praying. I said, "Well Lord, then start releasing that."

A few months later, I started hearing about some of the things that started to happen. During that same period of time, I was asking God about the book of Acts. I was reading through Acts 2 and one of the things I tend to do when I'm reading the Scriptures is I'm always looking to find out: "What's in there that we're supposed to be doing or supposed to be experiencing that we aren't doing yet?" Peter says on the day of Pentecost that when the Holy Spirit comes, "Your sons and your daughters are going to prophesy and they're going to dream dreams and see visions." "Well," I said, "we believe the Holy Spirit has been poured out on us, so why don't you release the dreams and visions?"

A month later, I was saying, "Lord, that's enough now. Do you think you could hold it back a little bit? I've got more dreams and visions than I know what to do with." They started to come. The giftings, the dreams, the prophetic ministry was already there – already given by the Lord – but until I opened my heart to it we weren't receiving it. Boom! Then it came. It started to be released. It's very interesting all the many different kinds of ways it has helped us in the last few years. Sometimes, God uses prophetic ministry to equip the people of God to do ministry. A lot of times, what prophetic people will do is call out the different things that God has already given us confirming our ministries so that we have the courage and the strength to press through to do those things.

We visited a church here in England and I had a prophetic guy with me. We were in a meeting and a young man came in late and our friend looked up at the young man and said, "There's Philip the Evangelist." The guy's name was Philip and he had an evangelistic call on his life. Needless to say, it got his attention instantly. Here's this person he's never met, calling him by name and telling him his ministry. Then he went on about how his evangelism was supposed to happen in the political arena, that God was calling him to go into politics to be an advocate for the poor. It devastated him because that had been his lifelong dream. He had begun to think that it wasn't godly enough and was going to walk away from it. Just at that moment, through the prophetic ministry, God intervened and said, "Hold on, you're about to throw away something valuable."

It also helps people to understand how much the Lord loves them, how much mercy he has for them. That's probably the thing we see the most often. It is also, I should add, something that can be used to reveal sins. We have a very quiet, little Asian lady in our church. She gets dreams, and one time she came to us and she had a list of about 12 people. God had revealed to her the secret sins of these 12 people. She said, "What am I supposed to do with this?" We looked at each other and we said, "Well, if there is anyone from whom they would want to hear their secret sins, it would probably be from her because she's the least intimidating person on the face of the earth." So we told her, "We want you to go to all 12 people and just share it with them and then ask them if that's right and then pray with them." So she did and every single one was right. Every single person responded, repented and prayed with her. So those are some of the things that are the benefits of prophetic ministry.

Let me just add one more important thing. Scripture is pretty clear; if you read in 1 Corinthians 13, the prophetic ministry that we have is imperfect. In some ways, it's not that much different from any of the other manifestations of God's presence and power. We live in this time of conflict between the kingdom of heaven and the kingdom of darkness and there is inconsistency. We pray for people. We see people healed. But we also pray for other people and they're not healed. We see people respond to the gospel and other people harden their hearts. The same thing is true of prophetic ministry. We see breakthroughs, powerful things happen and yet, there are mistakes that happen along the way and problems. How do you deal with it? The answer is in 1 Thessalonians 5:9.

It says, "Do not put out the Spirit's fire. Do not treat prophecies with contempt." Why would he even have to write that? Because obviously sometimes, they didn't turn out right or they caused difficulty. So he had to tell them, "Don't throw it all away just because there's a problem. Don't treat prophecies with contempt. Instead, he says in verse 21, "Test everything and hold on to the good." So one of the things we've had to do is develop a certain set of testing rules. You allow for people to test the prophecy so that it's not used to control, manipulate people or hurt people. One of the things we always encourage over again is that we do not have secret prophecies, where a prophetic person takes somebody off in a corner and gives them some word. It should be open where the body can test the validity – where, particularly, pastoral leadership can help people sort them out and deal with them. If this part is good and this part is not good, keep this part, throw this away: 'Well, we're not sure about this one, let's just put that on the shelf for a while' and so forth.

"She just said over and over again, 'I had no idea there was so much love.'"

Steve Nicholson *gives an illustration of prophecy*

A few years ago, I was in another city and a woman came up to me – she was obviously just new in the faith and she'd had a rough life. I was praying for her nose or some physical thing and she felt a little better. She said, "Thank you" and as she was walking away, this thought came into my mind. The Lord said to me, "Tell her that the baby she lost is with me and everything is OK." My first reaction was, "You've got to be kidding! I'm going to tell her that? What if it's wrong? I'm not going to say something like that." But then the Lord pressed me. "You're going to say it." Then I thought,"Well, I'm leaving town."

I just said, "Well, there is just one other thing." She came back and I said, "I just had this sense that there is a message God wanted to give to you and it was this – the baby you lost is with him and everything's OK." At first, she just stood there in stunned silence and said nothing. Finally, she broke down and began to pour out the story of how ten years previously, she'd had an abortion. When she had come to faith, the one thing she hadn't been able to feel forgiven for, and she was carrying this crushing weight of guilt about, was that baby. She just said over and over again, "I had no idea there was so much love. I had no idea there was so much power." It just broke through all those things in one fell swoop and cracked her heart wide open to how much Jesus really loved her. He loved her enough to give her that message just when she needed it. That's part of the point of the gift of prophecy.

"Jesus wants a bride who is absolutely in love with him."

John Arnott *on receiving the Holy Spirit*

It took me years to fully discover that a relationship with God wasn't merely about discovering truth but more about romance. Have you heard that God is love? We are called into intimacy with him. That's what he is after. Jesus doesn't simply want a group of people that will serve him. He could have made robots to do that. He wants a group of people that will be absolutely in love with him. He wants a bride that truly loves him. Do you blame him for that? How many young men want a bride that will love them? I sure do. What's the purpose of being married if there is no love in the marriage? That is what renewal is all about. But I didn't understand it at first.

I would say to Carol my wife, "Why can't I receive like you do?" and she would say, "I think it is because you are controlling." She meant that I would look at someone on the floor laughing and say, "I don't want to do that." A controlling person is always negotiating, always setting the terms of what the Holy Spirit can, or should or should not do. How many of you know that God wants to be God? The Lord wants to be the Lord. The boss. So we need to come to him like a little child and say, "Lord, whatever you want to do, I trust you enough. If you want to humble me; if you want to take me out of my comfort zone; if you want to fill me with joy or peace, or make me cry or whatever – I trust you and know that you'll turn it to good. Do whatever you want to do in my heart." That is really quite a statement. It is really risky.

I would always analyse everything. Analysis is a form of control. "I won't go along with it unless I understand." How many of you have said things like that? What we're doing is putting our own ability to analyse and understand as number one. Yet we read clearly that the natural mind does not understand the things of the Spirit of God. God is saying his ways are not our ways. We need to come into the place of intimacy. Revelation 2 says a lot about intimacy. For instance, God says to the church at Ephesus, "You do not love me as at first." People will, on the other hand, do all kinds of things that they don't understand because it feels good. What about kissing? There's only one reason for it – it feels good. Don't let people accuse you of being experience-oriented. There's more to marriage than experience and loving, however. You get up and go to work whether you feel like it or not. There's a whole practical side. Jesus has called us to love the Lord with all our hearts, soul, mind and strength, to enter into that place of intimacy. When the Holy Spirit comes and touches people powerfully and they fall down and cry or laugh or shake, perhaps they're just having a wonderful time with him. It doesn't need to make sense. You can check the fruit of the life afterwards.

"If you are going to be in love with someone you can love them without holding their hand – but it is nice to hold hands."

John Arnott *on the importance of focusing on God*

Let me talk about receiving the Spirit's power. In my experience, my wife Carol, would always receive the Holy Spirit very easily. She would fall down on the floor and would not be able to get up sometimes. Yet her heart was so yielded to the Lord that when he came on her the last thing she would ever say was, "No Lord." On the other hand, I was very unreceptive and would say, "I'm just not given to that sort of thing." I had been in the charismatic movement for 30 years and I know what it is to be pushed over by zealous ministry team people and evangelists. I would be braced on the inside thinking two things: (i) "This guy had better not push me," (ii) "Lord, I want the real thing. If this is not you God then I'm not going anywhere." I found out much later that my focus was totally in the wrong place. If you are going to receive from God, your focus needs to be on him.

Carol was so able to give her heart and love to the Lord that he would come and touch her every time. Meanwhile, I'm there analysing and evaluating myself and taking a reading on my balance. I would be saying, "Is this you Lord?" On the one hand, we don't really care about the manifestations but on the other, they are most precious and wonderful and sensitive. It is a way of your heart being touched by the Lord so that you know that you are dealing with something real. In other words, if you are going to be in love with someone, you can love them without holding their hand – but it is nice to hold hands. It is nice to experience the intimacy of that other person.

There are two dynamics – fear and pride. Fear will put control in place to ensure that you protect your heart. The way out of that is through repentance and moving into faith in a loving heavenly Father who would not give you a stone when you ask him for bread. The other is a pride that would put control in place. The way out of that is through humility and vulnerability which will lead to intimacy. I found these two things have been very important to my own understanding, and in helping many other people break through into having an experience with God that was very real and precious.

When the ministry team come and lay hands upon you and you receive a 'blessing' through the laying on of hands, it is like a jump start. It will get you going when you need help from your brothers and sisters. But the ideal place to experience the Lord, is you and him alone with the door shut where you just pour out your heart to him in secret. The bottom line of receiving from God is that there is something that calls out to him from the depth of your being that says, "Father I need you. I need to know your love. I want you. I'll seek you. I'll fast. I'll pray. I'll look for you in the secret place." I've noticed it's so dependent on hunger.

"It had never occurred to me that God was vulnerable..."

John Arnott *on intimacy with God*

The Lord said, "I will cause all my goodness to pass in front of you, and I will proclaim my name, the Lord in your presence. I will have mercy on whom I will have mercy, and I will have compassion on whom I will have compassion. But you cannot see my face, for no one may see me and live." Then the Lord said, "There is a place near me where you may stand on a rock. When my glory passes by, I will put you in a cleft in the rock and cover you with my hand until I have passed by. Then I will remove my hand and you will see my back but my face must not be seen." It's a wonderful picture of Jesus here. If you want to see the glory of God, if you want a revelation of who he is, you must hide in the cleft of the rock. The rock, Christ Jesus, has been split open for you and if you'll hide in him then the Father's presence will pass by and he'll show his glory.

Before this move of the Spirit started, the Lord told us he wanted our mornings, so we put those aside and we would pray and seek him. We were reading this same passage one morning and my heart cried out, "Oh God, why are you so hard to find? I want to see your glory. I'm hiding in Jesus," and just like that, he spoke back and said, "Because when I reveal my heart to people, I become very vulnerable." That hit me like a ton of bricks. It had never occurred to me that God was vulnerable at all. As I meditated on what he said, I realised that when someone comes close to you in intimacy, they extend their heart and it becomes very easy to hurt that person by responding in inappropriate ways. I began to realise that every time I felt God drawing near to me, I'd get my shopping list out and say, "Lord, I'm glad you're here. We need a new car and we need money for this... etc." I'd realise how I had hurt him whenever he desired me to come near to him in intimacy.

We wept and repented and cried together that day. Then the Lord spoke again and said, "Many of my people have married me for my money." I broke down again and said,"Lord I don't want you for your money. I don't want you for your power, your blessings or your gifts. I just want you for you. I want to have an intimate relationship with you." If that's what you want, that's what the Holy Spirit is offering. It's going to cost you your sophistication, your pride, your controlling fears.

"It is truly a 'time of refreshing come from the Lord.' "

Sandy Millar *answers the questions posed by the recent move of the Spirit*

We are in a very exciting time at the moment. Many people are being wonderfully touched by God. It is truly a 'time of refreshing come from the Lord.' (Acts 3:19) People are finding Christ – Christians are discovering a new love and fresh intimacy in their walk with God, new boldness and sense of direction in their lives, forgiveness, freedom, a new love for the Bible, a new concern for those whom God loves, those on the fringe of society, the poor, etc. and in many other ways experiencing closer communication with God. So who can complain about that and what are some of the principal things that are said to be wrong with it?

Firstly: **I don't like some of the manifestations.** It is not always put like that. The objections are usually couched in more apparently objective theological terms e.g. God wouldn't cause someone to do this or that – moo, roar, roll, etc. God wouldn't cause it and it is happening – it can't have been caused by God and must therefore (so the argument runs) be being caused by the devil.

In the first place, we need to emphasise again that it is not principally the manifestations on which we rely to authenticate a work of God. Prima facie, we believe that this current move is of the Spirit of God because he is now responding to the same prayer that we have always prayed. For many years now we have prayed, "Come, Holy Spirit" along the lines that Ezekiel was commanded to do in Ezekiel 37:9. He has come and we have been able to watch the fruit of that over the years. Use whatever biblical test you want to use – the generosity of the church members; their love for one another and 'the brethren'; their collective desire to serve God through ordination and more locally; their zeal in evangelism. I speak as a fool (2 Corinthians 11:21) but thousands of mainly unchurched people are going on an Alpha course somewhere around the country and the world each week, and most (it is worth repeating, *most*) come to Christ before the course is out. Alpha is a work of the Spirit and like most other works of the Spirit, it takes time for the fruit to grow. Of course, some of the manifestations may be of the flesh. Occasionally (but in our experience, it is much rarer than people might think) some may be of the devil. But just as you wouldn't feel safe in founding a biblical doctrine based only on one verse, so it is equally unsafe to express very settled views about manifestations based on only one visit to the church – and some of our more confident critics haven't even done that. The manifestations vary from time to time. I think it was John Wimber who was quoted as saying that if the price we pay for all this increase in the fruit of the Spirit is an occasional 'moo', it is a price worth paying.

Secondly: **These things all ended with Jesus, or the Apostles, or at the end of the Acts**, and therefore they can't be of God. This argument is one of those I described earlier as following a well-known path. There have always been those who think that signs and wonders (spiritual gifts, as we know them) are not for today. What I would say though, is it is important for us to see that a great deal of the criticism that is levelled at this current move of God's Spirit is in fact no more than a repetition of old and well-rehearsed arguments against a ministry of the Holy Spirit as we have always understood it.

The issues remain the same – nothing has changed since so-called 'Toronto' arrived. We are convinced that all the gifts, ministries and fruit of the Holy Spirit that we see in the New Testament remain a priority for the recovery of the church today. They did not, and were not intended to end with Jesus.

Thirdly: **This recent move of 'God' originated with X or Y; they were connected with Z. X, Y and/or Z hold heretical views in other areas, ergo this recent move of 'God' is based on heresy and can't be of God.** I am calling them X, Y and Z because it isn't always clear that the names are the same. The fallacy of the argument lies in the fact that the blessing of which we are speaking, comes direct from God and not from X, Y or Z. In our case, we learnt of what God is doing in other parts of the world from Eleanor Mumford. She simply taught us. How is anyone to hear about something (e.g. the gospel) if no one tells them? That doesn't mean that what we received was an 'Eleanor blessing'. She told us what God is doing elsewhere; she raised our faith and expectation and then prayed for us that GOD would pour out his Spirit and bless us in the same way. This is not a movement of God's Spirit associated with any one or group of teachers – that is one of its noticeable strengths. It is part of something God is doing all over the world. We are naturally interested in what others are teaching or saying elsewhere, but we shall continue to judge this move of God's Spirit along recognized New Testament principles in the light of what we see here and by what people here are experiencing.

Fourthly: **When the Holy Spirit really comes, there will be repentance, not laughter.** Our difficulty with this is that we cannot be sure what the laughter is caused by. What if it is an expression of the joy experienced in heaven over a sinner who has repented? Certainly, it is undeniable that we have seen a great deal of repentance as part of the more obvious and immediate fruit of this movement of God's Spirit – reconciliations, apologies, repentance as seen perhaps, most

obviously in the remarkable number of conversions in the
Alpha courses. I suspect this question is really expressing an
underlying uneasiness with laughter in church or possibly with
laughter in the kingdom of God at all. It is perfectly true that
laughter in the Bible often has negative connotations e.g. God
laughing at his enemies.

So the question we have to ask is: is it so far-fetched to
include laughter as an element in what is described in the Bible
as, "an inexpressible and glorious joy" (1 Peter 1:8)? A
banquet, a party with music and dancing ... (Luke 15:25)

I think not. Indeed, it is difficult to imagine an occasion of
such a joyful celebration in a Christian setting which wouldn't
feature a great deal of innocent laughter. So I think we come
round full circle. Those who have experienced this touch of
God's Spirit that inspires great and spontaneous laughter
(including myself) have found it an immensely refreshing
thing. It might not be the be-all and end-all of our Christian
experience but it certainly is a wonderful antidote to some of
what the Bishop of London called (in a different context) our
'po-faced' so-called spirituality. So let's keep laughing and
let's keep crying but above all, let's keep close to Jesus Christ
and to one another; let's make every allowance for our brethren
who find these things difficult but yield to none in our gratitude
for being alive in these times to see the beginning, as we hope
and pray this is, of the answer to the prayers of so many
Christians over so many years, who have cried out – "Oh God –
revive your church."

"I had to tell him to see because I saw that in the Bible!"

John Wimber *on healing*

I remember I was in Johannesburg, South Africa, and a man came up to me that had been born blind. He couldn't speak English – he was an Afrikaner and his wife was interpreting – and he said, "I understand that you heal blind people." I was out of resources at that moment and I remembered this text and thought, "Well, I've got a little bit of faith," and so we started praying for him. We didn't know when to stop. We didn't have any rules and so we kept saying to him, "Do you see anything? Do you see anything?" and he said, "No, no, no." He kept saying, "no" over and over again.

Now, "no" for an hour is a drag but we just kept asking, "Oh God, please heal this man. Give him his sight." Then all of a sudden, it popped into my head that I had to tell him to see because I saw that in the Bible! So I just said, "See," and all of a sudden he blinked up towards the lights above. I said, "What do you see?" and his wife said, "He doesn't know. He doesn't know what 'see' is." I said, "Why is his head tilted up?" and he said, "Something's up there." I said through her, "What is up there?" and he said, "I don't know but I counted and there's eight of them." Well, there were eight lights, four on each side hanging up there. "What do they look like?" Wrong words – how would he know?

So I realised that there had to be not only language translation but imaging translation. The brain had to learn to see.

But his eyes began rolling and we kept praying for him and pretty soon, he started reaching out, touching cheeks and foreheads and bodies and you knew that he was beginning to see. All of a sudden, I got images of little babies reaching out, touching their toes and finding their fingers – all the things that little babies do and I realised this guy in front of us who was about 60 years old, was learning to see. I almost fainted it was so incredible. I started saying, "He's learning to see," and he was crying, "Yes I know, I know."

When you see something like that, you have one part of your mind saying, "This ain't happening. It can't happen," and another part of your mind saying, "It's happening, it's happening alright, but I don't know why." You don't feel good enough. You don't feel Godly enough, but God will use his people to do his work.

"We've equated knowledge of God with having God."

John Wimber *on the importance of expecting God to intervene*

One of the difficulties we have today in the contemporary church is that we're so loaded up with information and ideas about God that we think we have God. Do you understand? We've equated knowledge of God with having God.

Let me put it in another context. If I were teaching you about sky-diving and I had a big board, and drew diagrams, talked about aerodynamics and how to get your suit on, what to do when you're jumping and what altitude you need to be at, what the best kind of plane is and what the best kind of clothing to wear is, and everybody got all their notebooks full – then I say, "Well, now you're sky-divers."

Somebody might raise their hand and say, "But don't we do it? Don't we have to get up in a plane and put on a uniform and test this theory out?" and I say, "No, it's enough that you just know that you can." You'd say, "Wait a minute. I didn't come to take this course just to learn about sky-diving. I came to take this course to be a sky-diver."

That is the problem today. We have Christians who know about Christ. We have Christians who have a great deal of information. They can make all the diagrams and fill in all the blanks at the appropriate place but they haven't ever jumped out of an aeroplane. They haven't allowed God to touch them. They don't walk in a daily way in which there's communication and flow and reality and relationship.

You could say to me, "Haven't you been saying that to us for a long time?" Yes. That's really the only message I have. Anything we talk about comes to that. Because I believe that what we have in the church today are people who have a theology that's based in theism but a practice that based in deism. By and large, most Christians today are deists – we don't really expect God to intervene or interact, especially when we're in a high-rise place with the air-conditioning on. How could God get around in those places and accommodate that kind of situation? We think God's confused by the advance in technology that we've brought about but, honestly he isn't. He's just as available now as he was in the time of his incarnational visit and we Christians need to know that.

"I don't make it look easy.
God makes it look easy."

John Wimber *on being natural in ministry*

At the root of most pastoral problems that I have dealt with – and we have a big church – is the basic assumption that, 'In my case God couldn't love me'. Someone came up to me once and said; "Will you pray for me for a blessing or for empowerment so that I can go and minister?" So I questioned them and out it came: "Well, I feel so powerless," and I laughed and said, "Well, that's the anointing. You don't understand. That's the way you are supposed to feel when you do God's stuff." Just how much of God's stuff can you do? Can you change one hair on your head? Can you add a cubit to your height? You can't even lose five pounds very readily!

I remember at one point David Watson [the English evangelist who died in 1984] was following me around, watching people getting healed and he said to me, "How do you do that?" I said, "Oh easy. Give me your hand," and I put his hand on a woman's eye that was blind and she saw. David walked around for the next hour staring at his hand and saying, "I did that, I did that. I participated in that."

I said, "Sure. What are they for if they are not for laying on people." He said, "But you make it look so easy." I replied, "I don't make it look easy. God makes it look easy. What do you want me to do – try to pretend it is hard? It's not hard. It's impossible."

My fat little freckled hands can't make something well. Think about it. How much can you add to God? What can you do in addition? Are you going to fall on your knees and pray harder? "Oh God, I've been such a sinner." He knows that. He's the one who saved you, remember? What are you going to add? I worked all that through a few years back and decided I don't have anything to add but what I can do is obey.

I don't have to float around like a butterfly and sting like a bee. I don't have to do something pretentious or stagey or theatrical. I don't have to raise my voice or act like I just came off from a mountain with a cloak over my shoulder. I decided a long time ago I wanted to multiply 'supernaturally natural' people. That meant I had to be natural.

"What I'm focused on is the major benefit: the church is being revitalised."

John Wimber *on the manifestations which sometimes accompany the move of the Spirit*

A young woman in our church came to me very lovingly, and said, "I'm about to have our baby." She had been married a couple of years and was pregnant and about to deliver. She said, "We would like you to come." I said, "To the delivery?" and she said, "Yes." I replied, "Honey, maybe I'm an old man but I don't want to know you that well. I don't want to participate in the birth of your child. I'll be happy to affirm you, love you, 'ooh' and 'aah' over the baby after it's born, but while it's being born I'd like to leave you to yourselves." She was quite puzzled by that and I realised that she was operating from a different set of assumptions about life than I am. I think we're all delighted with babies but I don't think many of us want to attend the birthing process.

I believe what we have in the church is a birthing process. I believe that the Holy Spirit has chosen to visit and revitalise the church and with it there are all kinds of noises and activities that would be best done behind closed doors. But church is an open activity and God has chosen to visit the church. I'm a little puzzled myself by some of the things that God chooses to reveal publicly but it happens that way, and so therefore I'm just one of those spectators too. I don't have any more explanation or idea of what it means than anybody else but I love the after-effect. Just as I love babies but am confused by the birthing process, I love what happens afterwards.

I talk to hundreds of young people in my own church as well as visitors. They tell me they love the Lord more and they read the Bible more. They're giving more and praying for the sick more, and they're operating in new gifts. Frankly, I don't care what the means is if it produces that benefit. What I'm focused on is the major benefit: the church is being revitalised. I was talking to two vicars and they've now had to open their church three additional times a week. Well, I think that's good news. I like that. That thrills me. It blesses me. So if somebody's got to make an animal noise to do that, I don't care. But I don't think it's anything we ought to legitimise and theologise, and emulate and try to get other people to do.

"It's like you've been cast in a role of Clark Kent."

John Wimber *on finding the 'phone booth' of faith*

You will be weak all your life in Christ for you can do nothing without him. On the other hand, you can do everything in him. We are always weak but appearing to be supermen and women. I was telling the young people in our church about this and I said, "It's like you've been cast in a role of Clark Kent. You're all Clark Kents but every now and then, you find the 'phone booth' of faith; you step into it and you emerge with your uniform on and do a mighty deed for Jesus." The kids took that literally in 1981 when we came to Chorleywood. We came a day or two early and were in Hyde Park when two of the young girls found a phone booth – one of those big cast-iron phone booths – went inside, 'found faith' and came out and started talking to people in the park.

The first person they talked to was a young Japanese student who couldn't speak much English. So they tried to explain salvation. They couldn't get much across but he liked the attention of two attractive young girls so he stayed there and listened. Finally, they asked him if they could pray for him and he didn't know what they meant but he said, "Yes." So they laid hands on him and he immediately fell down and began shaking violently. A crowd gathered because they were sure he was having an epileptic fit. They stood him back up and said, "Do you feel that?" and he said, "Ye-Ye-Ye-Ye-Yes." "Well, that's Jesus," they said.

So they led him to Christ in front of this group of 30 or 40 people. We have been called to a life of weakness and power. Isn't that an interesting paradox? We are asked to do such incredible things – heal the sick, cast out devils, feed the hungry, witness to the lost. Find the 'phone booth' of faith. It doesn't always look like a phone booth but find that spot of belief and say, "Lord, cause me to do in power what I can only do in weakness," and watch what happens.

Also edited by Mark Elsdon-Dew:

The God Who Changes Lives

"I went up to my bedroom with this terrible pain... I screamed, 'Oh God if you are there, do something...'"

"I had decided that my marriage was not recoverable and had left home..."

"I thought that if God was alive then he must be extraordinarily boring and certainly not worth getting to know..."

Does God act in people's lives today?

In this book, a variety of people describe how their lives have been transformed – often in dramatic circumstances – through an encounter with God. Some have been healed, some powerfully changed and others given the strength to face troubled times.

This is a book for anyone interested in whether God is there – and what he can do.

"There are some very beautiful stories in here, and they all serve to remind us that if the church is anything, it is about real people."

Methodist Recorder

"One of the great strengths of such a large number of testimonies is the variety. Drink, drugs, heavy metal music, Tarot, marriage breakdown, cot death and illness figure, together with the Lord's solution... It should prove a valuable addition to church bookstalls, and for giving to enquiring friends."

The Church of England Newspaper

Alpha Resources

The *Alpha* Course is a practical introduction to the Christian faith developed by Holy Trinity Brompton Church in London, England. *Alpha* Courses are now being run worldwide.

Alpha books by Nicky Gumbel:

- *Why Jesus?* A booklet recommended for all participants at the start of *Alpha*.

- *Why Christmas?* The Christmas version of *Why Jesus?*

- *Questions of Life* The *Alpha* Course in book form. In fifteen compelling chapters the author points the way to an authentic Christianity which is exciting and relevant to today's world.

- *Searching Issues* The seven issues most often raised by participants of *Alpha*: suffering, other religions, sex before marriage, the New Age, homosexuality, science and Christianity, and the Trinity.

- *A Life Worth Living* What happens after *Alpha*? Based on the book of Philippians, this is an invaluable next step for those who have just completed *Alpha*, and for anyone eager to put their faith on a firm biblical footing.

- *Challenging Lifestyle* An in-depth look at the Sermon on the Mount (Matthew 5-7). The author shows that Jesus' teaching flies in the face of modern lifestyle and presents us with a radical alternative.

- *Telling Others* This book includes the principles and practicalities of setting up and running *Alpha*. It also includes personal accounts of lives changed while attending *Alpha*.

Alpha Resources

Other resources available for setting up an *Alpha* Course:

- *Alpha* Introductory Video
- How to run an *Alpha* Course on Tape and How to run an *Alpha* Course on Video
- *Alpha* Team Training Tapes or Videos
- *Alpha* Team Training Manual (one for each small-group leader and helper)

Other resources available for running *Alpha*:

- The *Alpha* Course Tapes
- The *Alpha* Course Videos (5-video set including 15 talks)
- *Alpha* Manual (one for each small-group participant and leader)

Visit your local Christian bookshop or call the *Alpha* Hotline at STL for telephone orders: 0345 581278
(all calls at local rate – Please allow three working days for delivery)

In North America, all *Alpha* resources are published by Cook Ministry Resources, a division of Cook Communications Ministries.

In the USA, call or write:	In Canada, call or write:
Cook Ministry Resources	Beacon Distributing
4050 Lee Vance View	P.O. Box 98
Colorado Springs, CO 80918-7100	55 Woodslee Ave.
I -800-426-6596	Paris Ontario N3L 3E5
1-800-36-ALPHA (1-800-263-2664)	1-800-263-2664

For more information about *Alpha* please contact:

The *Alpha* Office, Holy Trinity Brompton,
Brompton Road, London SW7 IJA
Telephone: 0171 581 8255
Fax: 0171 584 8536
E-mail: HTB.LONDON@DIAL.PIPEX.COM